engage

The Bible gives us the big picture
In this issue of **engage** we'll see hu~ ~ess up those
plans, but we'll also see Jesus triu~ ~ing once and
for all. And we have thought-provoking articles to help
you make decisions, pray as you learn and share the gospel.

✱ DAILY READINGS Each day's
page throws you into the Bible, to
get you handling, questioning and
exploring God's message to you —
encouraging you to act on it and talk
to God more in prayer.

THIS ISSUE: Encouraging words
from **1 Thessalonians;** amazing
adventures in **Judges;** the mission
continues in **Acts;** darkness and light
in **Lamentations;** and wait for God's
day with **Zephaniah.**

✱ TAKE IT FURTHER If you're
hungry for more at the end of an
engage page, turn to the **Take it
further** section to dig deeper.

✱ REAL LIVES True stories,
revealing God at work in people's
lives. This time — **the man who
fought to abolish legal slavery.**

✱ TRICKY tackles those mind-
bendingly tricky questions that
confuse us all, as well as questions
our friends bombard us with. This
time: **Isn't living a good life
enough?**

✱ ESSENTIAL Articles on the
basics we really need to know about
God, the Bible and Christianity. This
issue, we look at what the Bible says
about **Jesus, the man.**

✱ STUFF Articles on stuff relevant
to the lives of young Christians. This
issue: **Making big decisions.**

✱ TOOLBOX is full of tools
to help you understand the Bible.
This issue we concentrate on **praying
about what you've read.**

All of us who work on **engage** are
passionate to see the Bible at
work in people's lives. Do you
want God's word to have an
impact on your life? Then open
your Bible, and start on the first
engage study right now...

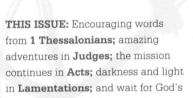

1 Set a time you can read the Bible every day

2 Find a place where you can be quiet and think

3 Grab your Bible, pen and a notebook

4 Ask God to help you understand what you read

5 Read the day's verses with engage, taking time to think about it

6 Pray about what you've read

BIBLE STUFF We use the NIV Bible version, so you might find it's the best one to use with engage. If the notes say **"1 Thessalonians 2 v 5–13"**, look up 1 Thessalonians in the contents page at the front of your Bible. It'll tell you which page the book starts on. Find chapter 2 of 1 Thessalonians, and then verse 5 of chapter 2 (the verse numbers are the tiny ones). Then start reading. Simple.

In this issue...

WHO TO BLAME FOR ENGAGE

Words and Bible stuff: Martin Cole Cassie Martin Carl Laferton Helen Thorne
Pics and design: Steve Devane
Proof-reading and heresy-spotting: Anne Woodcock Nicole Carter
The buck stops here: Martin Cole (martin@thegoodbook.co.uk)

1 Thessalonians

Ready for Jesus?

When Paul and Silas first visited the bustling port of Thessalonica, things didn't exactly go to plan. As usual, Paul went to the synagogue and told people about Jesus Christ. Many people became Christians, but the local Jews went haywire, started a riot and chased Paul and Silas out of town.

Despite this violent opposition, the church in Thessalonica grew. Paul wrote this letter to the Christians there, to encourage them to stick at it and to make sure they didn't give up or listen to any of the false teaching that surrounded them.

So who is this letter for?

New Christians – If you've not been a Christian long and are still fired up about it, this book is packed with advice and teaching just for you.

Finding it tough – If the Christian life is really hard for you, and you're wondering if you can go on, then read on. Paul was writing to Christians who were wobbling in their faith and needed to be put straight on a few things.

Strong Christians – Maybe you've been a Christian for years. Paul encourages such believers to get serious about God and about living for Him. It's time to sink your teeth into Paul's teaching, so you're ready for Jesus when He returns.

Non-Christians – If you're not a Christian or aren't sure if you are, 1 Thessalonians will put you straight. It outlines what Christianity is all about and why Jesus died and was raised back to life. It also tells us what life will be like as a Christian.

Whatever stage you're at, ask God to speak to you through this challenging and eye-opening letter. He will!

1 Christianity in conflict

The big city of Thessalonica had it all — sun, sea, sand and Caesar in charge. By the time Paul and Silas left, it was a story of synagogues, Scripture, scuffles and skedaddling.

👁 Read Acts 17 v 1–10

ENGAGE YOUR BRAIN

▷ *What did Paul preach about? (v3)*

▷ *What positive response did he receive? (v4)*

▷ *What did the Jews do? (v5–9)*

▷ *Why? (v5)*

Paul preached that Jesus is the Christ and the King of everything. He said it was no accident that He died on the cross — and that He'd come back from death. Paul, Silas and their friend Timothy had to leave Thessalonica and split up because of the trouble from the violent mob. When they met up again, Paul found out how the young Thess' Christians were doing, and decided to drop them a line...

👁 Read 1 Thessalonians 1 v 1–3

▷ *What should inspire growing Christians to work hard for God and stick with it? (v3)*

It's important to pray for other Christians, thanking God for them and asking Him to help them grow in their faith. Verse 3 also challenges our motives for serving God. Do you do good stuff to look impressive? Is it just duty? Or does your service spring from faith, hope and love?

PRAY ABOUT IT

Ask God to change your heart so you serve Him for the right reasons. Ask Him to help your hard work spring from faith in Him, love for Him and the certain hope of eternity with Jesus.

THE BOTTOM LINE

Serve God for the right reasons.

➡ TAKE IT FURTHER

Praytime — turn to page 108.

2 | Word power

Thessalonica was a tough place to be a Christian. Many other gods were worshipped, and much false religion was taught. And the Jews persecuted anyone who publicly followed Christ. And you think you've got it tough.

👁 Read 1 Thess 1 v 4–6

ENGAGE YOUR BRAIN
▶ How does Paul describe these believers? (v4)

▶ How did the gospel message reach them? (v5)

▶ How did they receive it? (v6)

Christians today share in the Thessalonians' experience. All believers have been chosen by God and are loved by Him. The message of Jesus comes to us with words (explaining the gospel), with power (from God, challenging us), with the Holy Spirit (helping us understand it) and with conviction (from people convinced of the gospel). We should try to live like those who shared the gospel with us, and receive it with joy.

👁 Read verses 7–10
▶ What was remarkable about these Christians? (v8)

▶ How should Christians' lives change? (v9)

▶ What should Christians be doing now? (v10)

Verse 10 mentions God's wrath. He's angry with people for turning away from Him. But v10 also says that those who trust in Jesus will be rescued from God's future judgment. Great news!

GET ON WITH IT
▶ How can the Lord's message ring out (v8) from you?

PRAY ABOUT IT
Ask God to help you turn away from the idols in your life; and to shout out His message all around you; and to wait and be ready for Jesus' return.

→ TAKE IT FURTHER
Imitation Engage on page 108.

3

Fair share

Paul and Silas had fled from Thessalonica fearing for their lives. But it wasn't a hit-and-run gospel attack from Paul. He stayed in touch with the Christians in that city, encouraging them and seeing them grow in their faith.

👁 Read 1 Thess 2 v 1–6

ENGAGE YOUR BRAIN

▶ *How was Paul able to share the gospel in such hostile circumstances? (v2)*

▶ *What shouldn't we do when we share the gospel? (v3–5)*

▶ *What should be our motive? (v4)*

Talking to people about Jesus can often be a tricky task in the face of angry opposition. We shouldn't be tempted to resort to trickery or flattery. We must tell it how it is, doing it to please God, not out of selfish motives.

👁 Read verses 7–12

▶ *What did Paul and friends do while in Thessalonica? (v8–9)*

▶ *How did they treat the people they met? (v7, v11)*

▶ *What did this involve? (v12)*

As Christians, we have a responsibility to share the gospel — the good news about Jesus. That doesn't merely mean talking about Jesus: we must also live in a way that honours God (v10). We shouldn't bash people over the head with Bible truths, but be loving and caring towards them. Sharing our lives with them, as well as the gospel. Being a Christian is a whole lifestyle — living for God — it's not hit-and-run Bible bashing. God wants us to comfort people and encourage them to live for Him (v12).

GET ON WITH IT

▶ *How will you change the way you share the gospel and the way you behave around non-Christians?*

▶ *Who will you comfort, encourage, & share your life with this week?*

THE BOTTOM LINE

It's all about pleasing God, not making a name for ourselves.

→ TAKE IT FURTHER

Get your fair share on page 108.

4 | Word's worth

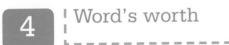

"I'm scared of sharing my faith with people. Why should anyone listen to my words and beliefs?" The great news is that it's not our words that bring people to Jesus...

👁 Read 1 Thess 2 v 13–14

ENGAGE YOUR BRAIN

▷ *What did these guys recognise about the message Paul gave them? (v13)*

▷ *What's the proof they'd accepted the truth about Jesus? (v14)*

It's not our words that change people's lives. It's true that God can use us to do amazing things. But it's His word — the awesome message of Jesus — that changes lives, not anything we do.

If someone truly accepts the gospel, we'll see it at work in their lives. We'll see them living for God, just as other believers do.

👁 Read verses 14–16

▷ *What did these enemies of God do? (v14–16)*

▷ *What were they trying to stop? (v16)*

▷ *Would God tolerate this?*

The enemy can seem terrifying at times. Satan inspired a group of Jews to kill Jesus; he stirred up people to destroy the church in Thessalonica; and he wants to stop you from spreading the gospel. But God's in control — His punishment (wrath) will come to anyone who fights against the gospel (v16). When opposition seems to much for us, we must remember that God is on our side and He will defeat His enemies.

THINK IT THROUGH

▷ *How do v13–16 encourage you?*

▷ *How will this affect the way you share the gospel?*

THE BOTTOM LINE

It's not down to us; it's God who changes lives and punishes sin.

→ TAKE IT FURTHER

Words of wrath on page 108.

5 | Missing people

Is there anyone you're far away from, who you wish you could spend more time with? Paul missed these young Christians and wished he was with them.

👁 Read 1 Thess 2 v 17–20

ENGAGE YOUR BRAIN

▶ Why was Paul so keen on visiting these believers? (v19–20)

▶ What stopped him? (v18)

Paul suffered loads for spreading the message about Jesus. But he knew it was more than worth it — he would be rewarded with eternal life with Jesus. And he took great joy in knowing these Christians in Thessalonica would share in it too, despite all the odds against them.

👁 Read 1 Thess 3 v 1–5

▶ Why did Paul send Timothy to them? (v2–3)

▶ Why shouldn't they worry about Paul? (v3–4)

▶ What had Paul been worried about? (v5)

When someone becomes a Christian, we can't just leave them to it and expect them to grow and mature. Young Christians need to be encouraged, taught and helped through tough times, so they grow and aren't tempted away from Jesus.

GET ON WITH IT

▶ Which younger Christians will you get alongside and encourage?

▶ Which older Christian can you ask to do the same for you?

It's no good simply hoping for the best, or leaving it to God to look after new Christians. If we care like Paul, we won't be able to rest until we're sure all is well.

PRAY ABOUT IT

Spend time praying for young Christians you know. How about sending them an encouraging email or visiting them?

➔ TAKE IT FURTHER

Get emotional on page 108.

6 ¦ Thessalonian thrill

Do you pray much? What do you pray about? Who do you pray for? How often do you pray for other Christians? It's time for some prayer pointers from Paul.

👁 **Read 1 Thess 3 v 6–13**

ENGAGE YOUR BRAIN

▷ *What encouraged Paul? (v7)*

▷ *What made him happy? (v9)*

▷ *What two things did he long to do? (v10)*

Paul and his friends were so encouraged to hear how the Christians in Thessalonica were growing in faith, despite facing great opposition. The news breathed new life into Paul, Timothy and the others (v8). They wanted to visit these guys and help them grow even more in their faith.

THINK IT THROUGH

▷ *Are you pleased and encouraged when you hear about other Christians doing well?*

▷ *Or do you get jealous or just not care?*

👁 **Read verses 11–13**

▷ *What does Paul pray for these Christians?*

v12:

v13:

PRAY ABOUT IT

Paul prays that he'll be able to meet and encourage those Christians. He asks God to make these guys overflow with love for each other. And he prays they'll be strengthened and become more holy.

Below, list several Christians you know. Include some who live far away and some you don't get along with:

-
-
-
-
-

Use v11–13 to start you off praying for each one of them in turn.

→ TAKE IT FURTHER

Visiting time on page 109.

7 | Let's talk about, umm, thingy

Sex. Christians rarely talk about it. We tend to blush and brush it under the carpet, just assuming we all behave sex-wise. But sex stuff causes problems for Christians too, and Paul knew it.

👁 Read 1 Thess 4 v 1–8

ENGAGE YOUR BRAIN
- ▶ *What should we be aiming for? (v1, v7)*
- ▶ *What help does God give us? (v8)*

Sexual self-control isn't easy, but we're not on our own — God's Spirit lives in all believers, helping them to please Him.

- ▶ *Why should we bother? (v3a)*
- ▶ *What does God expect us to do? (v4)*
- ▶ *Who else can sexual sin affect? (v6)*
- ▶ *What's the bad news for those who disobey and reject God? (v6)*

It's time to get honest with yourself and with God...

GET ON WITH IT
- ▶ *How's your self-control?*
- ▶ *When it comes to sex, what areas do you struggle with? Porn? Lustful thoughts or actions?*

- ▶ *How do the things you say dishonour God, in the area of sex?*
- ▶ *How do your attitudes to sex and relationships need to change?*
- ▶ *Be honest — what do you need to sort out?*

TALK IT OVER
If you do have a problem you want to deal with, you should talk to someone. An older Christian or a Christian friend who can help you and who will challenge you and ask how you're getting along. Yes, it's embarrassing, but it's essential.

PRAY ABOUT IT
Time to talk these things over with God, being open, honest and asking for His help. And pray for friends who struggle too.

THE BOTTOM LINE
"Avoid sexual immorality" (v3)

→ TAKE IT FURTHER
More sex talk on page 109.

8 More love, less noise!

**How good are you at loving other Christians?
Do you live a quiet life or are you always making
yourself look good? Do you work hard?
Do non-believers respect you for the way you live?**

👁 Read 1 Thess 4 v 9–10

ENGAGE YOUR BRAIN
▶ *What were these Christians great at? (v9)*

▶ *Yet what does Paul say they should do? (v10)*

Whether you're great at showing love to others, or rubbish at it... you can never do it too much. We can always be more loving — in our words, actions and even thoughts.

GET ON WITH IT
▶ *Who do you need to be more loving towards?*

▶ *So what are you going to do?*

👁 Read verses 11–12
▶ *What two surprising ambitions does Paul say they should have?*

▶ *Why should they aim for these things?*

It seems that these Christians were so excited about Jesus returning, they'd stopped working, got lazy, became annoyingly loud and were being busybodies! Wealthy Greeks often gave up manual work. But Paul said this was dangerous. They should stop poking their noses into other people's business and work hard to win the respect of outsiders to Christianity.

PRAY ABOUT IT
What has God challenged you about today? Talk it over with Him now.

THE BOTTOM LINE
Love others and work hard so God gets the glory.

→ TAKE IT FURTHER
More stuff on page 109.

9 | Back to the future

Are you excited about the future? Paul was! Check out how excited he got when talking about the most important event in the future — the second coming of Jesus Christ.

For the church in Thessalonica, the explanation about what was going to happen couldn't come soon enough. They were worried about their Christian friends who'd died. Where were they exactly? What would happen to them when Jesus returned? Paul now gives them, and us, a clear view of what's to come. To learn what the future holds, we must get back to the Bible.

👁 Read 1 Thess 4 v 13–14

ENGAGE YOUR BRAIN
▶ *What happened to Jesus?*

▶ *So what does this mean for Christians who have died? (v14)*

Notice the great way he describes them — they're asleep in Jesus. There is no need to grieve over them as you would unbelievers, for they are totally safe with their Saviour. And their resurrection is just as certain as Jesus' own, because they're *"in Jesus"*.

👁 Read verses 15–18
▶ *What will happen when Jesus returns? (v16–17)*

▶ *What's the incredible result for Christians? (end of v17)*

▶ *What should we do with this knowledge? (v18)*

People have different opinions about what will happen when Jesus returns and what exactly will happen before then. But we shouldn't worry about that — if it was vital to know, the Bible would make it clear to us. We do know that it will be spectacular (v16). The most important fact is that Jesus will gather all believers and they'll be with Him forever (v17) That's worth shouting about!

GET ON WITH IT
▶ *How will you encourage Christian friends with these verses?*

➡ TAKE IT FURTHER
Face death on page 109.

10 Day return

When exactly is Jesus coming back? And will we be OK when He does? What should we be doing in the meantime? Paul gives us some clear answers to these big questions.

👁 Read 1 Thess 5 v 1–5

ENGAGE YOUR BRAIN

- ▶ *What did Paul say about the date of Jesus' return? (v1–2)*
- ▶ *Who will it catch by surprise? (v3)*
- ▶ *Why will it be different for Christians?*

We don't know exactly when Jesus will return, so there's no point trying to work it out. We must make sure we're ready for it, living in the light — serving Him. It will be a great day for Christians, but a horrific shock for people who've rejected Jesus (v3).

👁 Read verses 6–11

Paul uses the *"sleep"* in different ways here: v6 = ignoring Jesus, v7 = natural sleep, v10 = death.

- ▶ *So how should Christians be different? (v6, v8)*
- ▶ *So what should we actually do about it? (v11)*
- ▶ *What's the brilliant news for believers? (v9–10)*

Jesus' death achieved incredible things for us. He rescued us from God's anger and punishment for our sin. So when Jesus does return, Christians will go to live with Him. This great news should spur us on to live differently from those who reject Jesus.

GET ON WITH IT

- ▶ *How should you be more self-controlled?*
- ▶ *How can your faith and love and hope in Jesus be more obvious in your life?*
- ▶ *Who will you build up with v9–10?*

PRAY ABOUT IT

Ask God to help you do these things, so that you're ready for Jesus when He returns.

→ TAKE IT FURTHER

Return to the *Take it further* section on page 109.

11 | Check it out

As he gets towards the end of his letter, Paul gives the Thessalonians a final checklist to make sure they're ready for Jesus' return. Two things they need to look at: their relationship with others and their relationship with God.

👁 Read 1 Thess 5 v 12–15

To be ready for Jesus, our relationships with others have to be good. Are there any friendships you need to sort out before Jesus returns?

GET ON WITH IT

Think of:

a) one way you could show more respect for your Christian leaders.

b) one friend, timid in their faith, whom you could encourage.

c) one person you could be more patient and kind with.

👁 Read verses 16–18

GET ON WITH IT

▶ *Are you happy about your life and what Jesus has done for you?*

▶ *How can you be more joyful?*

▶ *What will you do to make sure you pray loads?*

Now make a list of some of the things you can thank God for:

-
-
-
-
-
-
-
-

PRAY ABOUT IT

Read the verses again and talk to God about the bits that hit you hardest.

THE BOTTOM LINE

Respect your leaders. Encourage timid Christians. Be kind. Be happy! Pray all the time. Be thankful.

→ TAKE IT FURTHER

Check out page 110.

12 | Goodbye and God bless

It's time for Paul to sign off. He has a few more words of advice and encouragement before he finishes. Before you read these verses, ask God to challenge and encourage you through them.

👁 Read 1 Thess 5 v 19–22

ENGAGE YOUR BRAIN
▣ What should we do with all the teaching we hear and read?

Verses 19–20 are saying: don't quench what God is teaching through His word. Take it on board, don't despise it or treat it lightly. And test everything you hear — is it in line with what the Bible teaches? If so, treasure it and live by it. And stay away from evil influences in your life.

👁 Read verses 23–28
▣ How would you summarise Paul's prayer for these Christians? (v23)

▣ What is Paul confident about? (v24)

▣ What does he ask the Thessalonians to do? (v25–27)

GET ON WITH IT
▣ Do you pray for Christians who teach and encourage you?
▣ Who could you pray for?

▣ Who will you ask to pray for you?

▣ Who could you read the Bible with? (v27)

PRAY ABOUT IT
Which Christians will you commit to praying more for? Start now, using v23–24 to kick you off.

→ TAKE IT FURTHER
Last look at this letter on page 110.

15

Making big decisions

Life is full of decisions — big, life-changing ones (What job? Who to marry?) and smaller, everyday ones (What socks? Whose hairstyle to copy?). And life is full of people offering guidance: friends, family, fortune-tellers, and so on. What about God? Does He offer us guidance? How does He do it?

GOD'S PRIORITIES

When my wife goes away, she gives me lots of guidance about how to wash my clothes and how to cook. She doesn't advise me about what to watch on TV. That's how I know what her priorities are: it's what she gives me guidance about.

So, what are God's priorities for us, the things He gives us guidance about?

Priority One — God wants us to be *"wise for salvation through faith in Christ Jesus"* (2 Timothy 3 v 15). God's top priority is your salvation. He wants you to put your faith in His Son, Christ Jesus, so that you can enjoy eternal life.

Priority Two — *"It is God's will that you should be sanctified"* (1 Thessalonians 4 v 3). "Sanctified" means "purified", or "cleaned". God wants you to live a life that isn't dirtied by sin — in other words, to become the person He made you to be.

Salvation and sanctification: these are the things God cares most about, and so it's in those areas that He gives us guidance.

GOD'S GUIDANCE

When my wife's away, she leaves me notes. Her words give me the guidance I need to do what she considers important.

And God's words give us all the guidance we need to do what He considers are the priorities for our life.

16

So, *"the Holy Scriptures ... are able to make you wise for salvation through faith in Christ Jesus"*, because *"all Scripture is God-breathed"* (2 Timothy 3 v 15–16). God gives us instruction on salvation in Scripture (the Bible).

And because all of Scripture is written by God, it *"is useful for teaching, rebuking, correcting and training in righteousness, so that the man of God may be thoroughly equipped for every good work"* (2 Timothy 3 v 16–17). God guides us about how to be sanctified, how to do good works, through His word.

The point is this — God's guidance for us is found in His word, the Bible. And all of the guidance we need is found in the Bible.

We don't need to wait for booming heavenly voices or strange dreams to guide us: we have all we need in God's word. And if we do think God's spoken to us in a different way, we can compare that with what the Bible teaches, because that's where we know for sure that God is guiding.

Equally, there are many things Scripture is silent about. God hasn't told us exactly what job to do; exactly who to marry; precisely which church to go to. But He does guide us about how to do our work, what kind of person to marry, what to look for in a church, so that we'll keep our SALVATION (faith in Jesus) and grow in SANCTIFICATION (becoming the people we were made to be).

YOUR WORD IN MY HEART

The Bible encourages us to be like an ancient member of God's people, who wrote: *"How can a young man keep his way pure? By living according to your word ... I have hidden your word in my heart that I might not sin against you"* (Psalm 119 v 9, 11). When we want to know how God wants us to live, we need to know what He says in His word; we need to remember it; and we need to get on with obeying it.

Judges

Heroes and zeroes

It's a book about judges. No surprises there. But not the kind who hang out in court all day — these were action-packed rescuers. Picked by God and helped by His Spirit to rescue God's people, the Israelites.

Judges continues the Old Testament story of God and His people. So what happened before Judges? Well, the people God created in the beginning lived in the Garden of Eden, under His command and care. It was perfect — God's people in God's place living under His rule. But Adam and Eve rejected God's rule and turned against Him, earning His anger and punishment. Booted out of Eden, they lost that perfect, face-to-face relationship with God.

But it wasn't all over. God's plan, formed before creation, was to reveal the depths of His love: He launched a rescue mission. In time, God's people would worship Him not just because He created them, but because He'd won them back. God promised to reverse the effects of His people's rebellion against Him. He said He'd do that by choosing a people (starting with Abraham) who'd belong to Him and benefit from Him. He promised to bless the world through His people.

God rescued them from slavery in Egypt and made sure they got to the land He'd promised them, Canaan — despite huge obstacles on the way which would make them rely on Him. Under Joshua, they conquered the land, kicked out its occupants and life began to look good for the Israelites.

Would it continue that way or would they hit a depressing downward spiral? And how does all this point us to the ultimate Rescuer, Jesus? There's only one way to find out. Get ready for loads of action in one of the wildest books in the Bible...

13 So far, so good

Moses and the Israelites had disobeyed God and failed to conquer Canaan. So they were punished, wandering the desert for 40 years until the whole generation had died out. But life was more successful with Joshua in charge...

👁 **Read Joshua 21 v 43–45**

ENGAGE YOUR BRAIN

▷ *What did God give to His people?*

▷ *How had God failed them? (v45)*

Life was awesome. God kept all His promises and gave His people great victories as they conquered the promised land. They were God's people, living in His land, under His rule. Then Joshua died...

👁 **Read Judges 1 v 1–10**

▷ *Which Israelite tribes fought these great battles? (v3)*

▷ *Who really won the battles? (v4)*

▷ *Why didn't Adoni-Bezek complain about his horrific torture? (v6–7)*

👁 **Read verses 11–15**

▷ *Who took up Caleb's challenge?*

▷ *What was his reward?*

(Remember the name Othniel – he'll be big news in chapter 3.) So far, so good for the Israelites. They're obeying God and He's given them great victories, including conquering Jerusalem, which would become the main city for God and His people.

In the Old Testament, God seems to punish people loads. But notice that when His people loyally obey Him, He keeps His amazing promises and gives them great rewards. Tomorrow, we'll see what happens when people are casual with God's commands.

PRAY ABOUT IT

Think of some of God's great promises to His people. Thank Him that He always keeps His word and gives His people great things.

THE BOTTOM LINE

God always keeps His promises.

→ **TAKE IT FURTHER**

A little bit more on page 110.

14 | Total wipeout?

Yesterday we saw the Israelites get off to a good start in Canaan — God giving them victory over their enemies as they conquered loads of territory. They were obeying their great God. But how long would it last?

👁 Read Judges 1 v 16–21

ENGAGE YOUR BRAIN

▷ *Who was behind these successes?*
▷ *What went wrong? (v19, v21)*

This may not seem so bad. But God had commanded His people to drive out all His enemies from the land He was giving them (Numbers 33 v 52). If they failed to do this, they'd be turned against God by these people (Exodus 23 v 33). This was serious stuff – there was no room for failure.

👁 Read verses 22–36

▷ *Which of the twelve Israelite tribes failed to complete the job?*
   v19:
   v21:
   v27–28:
   v29:
   v30:
   v31–32:
   v33:
   v34:
   v35:

There were some great victories, but most of the Israelite tribes didn't fully carry out God's commands. They thought they'd done enough and seemed happy to live alongside their enemies. Sometimes we think we've made good progress in the Christian life and can relax a bit. We can afford to leave some areas only partly dealt with. Remember that sliding away always starts gently...

THINK IT THROUGH

▷ *Which sins do you lazily leave in your life?*
▷ *What do you need to do about it?*

PRAY ABOUT IT

Some things seem too hard for us to deal with. But we're not alone — God wants to help us fight our sin enemies. Ask Him to help you in your battles. Mention the specific sin enemies you can't seem to beat.

→ TAKE IT FURTHER

No *Take it further* today.

15 Round and round

The people of Israel conquered Canaan, but didn't make a thorough job of it. They didn't clear all the locals out. And they soon found that where there was a Canaanite, there was a Canaanite god as well. Disaster loomed.

👁 **Read Judges 2 v 1–5**

ENGAGE YOUR BRAIN

▷ *Where did they go wrong? (v2)*

▷ *Why shouldn't they have done this? (v1)*

▷ *What would be the result? (v3)*

👁 **Read verses 6–15**

▷ *What were the Israelites like when Joshua was around? (v7)*

▷ *What about the next generation? (v10–12)*

▷ *What happened to them? (v14–15)*

👁 **Read verses 16–23**

▷ *What great thing did God do for His disobedient people? (v16)*

▷ *How did they respond? (v17)*

▷ *What did God do next and why? (v20–22)*

There's a big pattern running through the book of Judges:

God's people turn to other gods

God lets their enemies defeat them

Israelites cry out to God

God sends a judge to rescue them

PRAY ABOUT IT
- Confess your current sins to God.
- Thank Him that He's totally fair and punishes sin.
- Cry out to Him to rescue you and help you fight the sin in your life.
- Thank Him for sending His Son to rescue you once and for all.

⮕ **TAKE IT FURTHER**
Go round to page 110.

21

16 | Judge number one

"We're in the book of Judges, but we haven't met a judge yet!" I hear you (almost) cry. Well, today we'll briefly get acquainted with Israel's first judge sent by God to rescue them. Actually we've met him before...

👁 Read Judges 1 v 11–13

👁 Then read Judges 3 v 7–11

Yesterday we read chapter 2, which outlined the whole of Judges. This pattern occurs again and again.

God's people turn to other gods

God lets their enemies defeat them

Israelites cry out to God

God sends a judge to rescue them

ENGAGE YOUR BRAIN

Check how Othniel's story fits the pattern:

🔹 *What did God's people do wrong? (v7)*
🔹 *How did God punish them? (v8)*
🔹 *So what did the Israelites do? (v9)*
🔹 *So what did God do? (v9)*

🔹 *How was Othniel able to rescue God's people? (v10)*
🔹 *So what did God bring to His undeserving people? (v11)*

When His people cried out to Him, God rescued them. Even though they deserved to be wiped out for the way they'd treated Him. And God will rescue anyone who cries out to Him to rescue them from their sin.

It was God who gave Othniel the power to save the Israelites. Life may seem impossible sometimes, but God is in control. Only He has the power to defeat sin and win the victory for His people.

PRAY ABOUT IT

Think about what this short story tells us about God and His people. Let this influence your prayers as you talk to God now.

→ TAKE IT FURTHER

More stuff on page 110.

17 | Eglon his fat face

As judges go, Othniel was quite normal.
Today we read about a much stranger character.
Get ready for one of the weirdest, most exciting
and disgusting stories in the Bible.

👁 **Read Judges 3 v 12–23**

ENGAGE YOUR BRAIN

▷ *How is the circular pattern of Judges shown again in v12–15?*

▷ *What opportunity did Ehud use to get to fat King Eglon?*

The Israelites were invaded by enemies again after turning away from God. After 18 years, they cried to God for help and He gave them lefty Ehud to deliver (rescue) them. And what a way to do it. And look at the pointed message he gave to chubby Eglon from God (v20).

👁 **Read verse 24–30**

▷ *What did Eglon's assassination lead to? (v27–29)*

▷ *What was the great result for God's people? (v30)*

This weird tale is all about God using an unusual rescuer who uses strange ways to save people. As we'll see

through the rest of Judges (and the whole Old Testament), God continued to use unusual rescuers to save His people in surprising ways.

THINK ABOUT IT

▷ *Who was the most unusual rescuer of all time?*

▷ *And in what surprising way did He save people? (Check out Romans 5 v 8)*

PRAY ABOUT IT

Thank God that He can use weirdos like us to serve Him in amazing ways. And thank Him for the perfect Rescuer He sent to save us — Jesus.

THE BOTTOM LINE

God uses surprising methods to rescue His people.

➔ **TAKE IT FURTHER**

For the next judge, turn to page 111.

18 Here come the girls

After Ehud and 80 years of peace, the Israelites were back to their old, evil ways. Get ready for another surprising rescuer and more disgusting deaths.

👁 Read Judges 4 v 1–16

ENGAGE YOUR BRAIN

▷ *In which verses do you see the same old Israelite pattern?*

▷ *What were God's people up against? (v2–3)*

▷ *What was surprising about God's next hero? (v4)*

▷ *What did God promise to do, using Barak? (v6–7)*

▷ *What was Barak's response? (v8)*

▷ *How was Deborah's response different? (v14)*

▷ *What happened and who was behind it? (v16)*

👁 Read verses 17–24

▷ *What happened to Sisera? (v21)*

▷ *What did God do for His people? (v23–24)*

Another gruesome death. And yet again God used surprising people and unusual methods to rescue His people. God used two women and a nervous wreck to conquer a mighty enemy with 900 iron chariots! God's rescue is always impressive and perfect, even if the methods seem weird at the time.

And He has patience with timid believers like Barak. Look at the huge difference between verses 8 and 14. Barack was transformed by God from cowardly to courageous.

PRAY ABOUT IT

Thank God for His patience in developing your feeble faith. Ask Him to give you the confidence and belief to serve Him courageously.

➡ TAKE IT FURTHER

More about Barak on page 111.

19 Deborah: The Musical

Yesterday we read the amazing story of Deborah the prophetess, nevous Barak, iron chariots and death by tent peg. Now imagine putting all that into a song.

👁 Read Judges 5 v 1–11

ENGAGE YOUR BRAIN

▷ *How many times is "the Lord" mentioned in these verses?*

▷ *Why do you think that is?*

▷ *What happened when the people deserted God? (v8)*

Deborah is singing about how tough life had been — it wasn't safe to travel on the roads (v6); the Israelites couldn't defend themselves (v8). Then God rescued them and their lives changed dramatically. That's why the Lord gets so many mentions.

👁 Read verses 12–23

▷ *Who fought alongside Deborah and Barak?*

▷ *And who wimped out and stayed at home?*

▷ *What "good" reasons do you use to avoid doing what God wants?*

Verse 20 probably means that God used the skies to defeat the enemy. He caused rain and a flooded river (v21) to drown them. God was the real hero here.

👁 Read verses 24–31

▷ *Jael did something horrifically violent — so why was she praised so highly?*

▷ *What two things did Deborah pray? (v31)*

PRAY ABOUT IT

Will you pray that God's enemies are defeated? And how about praying for Christians you know, that they'll serve God more and more.

THE BOTTOM LINE

God rescues His people.
Sing His praises.

→ TAKE IT FURTHER

Wander off to page 111.

20 | Invaded

Yesterday we saw the Israelites singing God's praises, but after a while they were singing the same old tune and forgetting the Lord. So their singing would turn to cries again.

👁 Read Judges 6 v 1–6

▶ How impressive was the Israelites' enemy this time? (v5)

▶ What did they do to Israel? (v3–4)

▶ What were God's people reduced to doing? (v2)

▶ What did they eventually get around to doing? (v6)

Imagine this invasion, destruction and terror for 7 years in a row. But it was exactly what they deserved for turning away from God. Eventually, they turned back to Him for help.

👁 Read verses 7–10

▶ Did God send a judge immediately to rescue His people?

▶ What had God done in the past for them? (v8–9)

▶ What had He asked the Israelites to do? (v10)

God's people asked for a rescuer, but instead He sent a prophet to tell them off. They needed more than just a quick fix — their sin problem was long term. They needed to realise they were suffering because they'd turned their backs on God.

We often bring a shopping list of requests to God in prayer, and yet forget our responsibilities in living for Him. One of the kindest things God does for us is to show us exactly how we're messing up. With His help, we can put things right and start living for Him again.

PRAY ABOUT IT

Don't forget to listen to what God is teaching you. Ask Him to show you your sin and how to sort it out. And then bring your other requests to God. Try it now.

→ TAKE IT FURTHER

More prayer tips on page 111.

21 Mighty weakling

Today we meet a mighty warrior. But if he's so mighty, why does he claim to be the least important person from the weakest family? And why is he hiding in a winepress?

👁 Read Judges 6 v 11–16

ENGAGE YOUR BRAIN

▷ *How did the angel, representing God, greet Gideon? (v12)*

▷ *What was Gideon's less than friendly answer? (v13)*

▷ *How have v8–10 already answered this?*

▷ *So how would God rescue Israel this time? (v14)*

▷ *How could weakling Gideon possibly do that? (v16)*

Gideon has loads of questions and many doubts. But God has just one answer for him: *"I will be with you"* (v12, v16). This great promise will help us keep going through many bad times. God doesn't answer all of Gideon's questions or fill in all the details. Faith in God, knowing that He will be with us, should be enough.

👁 Read verses 17–24

▷ *What impressive thing did the angel do? (v21)*

▷ *Why was Gideon terrified? (v22)*

Gideon realised he was in the presence of all-powerful, almighty God. Sometimes we forget how impressive and terrifying God is. This is the Creator of the universe. No wonder Gideon freaked out. Yet the Lord promised to keep Gideon safe.

PRAY ABOUT IT

This is the God we serve. This is the God who's on our side. He is awesome and loving and powerful and forgiving. When you talk to God, do you give Him the respect He deserves? Why not start right now?

THE BOTTOM LINE

Almighty God is with His people.

→ TAKE IT FURTHER

Find more on page 112.

22 | Choosing sides

God has chosen nervous Gideon to rescue His people. Yesterday we saw Gideon build an altar for God. But the town already has an altar — to the false god Baal.

Read Judges 6 v 25–32

▷ What was God's first task for Gideon?

▷ Is Gideon looking like a mighty warrior yet? (v27)

▷ What did the locals think of Gideon's demolition job? (v28–30)

▷ What was Gid's dad's brilliant answer to this murderous mob? (v31)

God commanded Gideon to tear down the altar used for worshipping other gods like Baal. God's message to Israel was this: you can't worship both me *and* other gods. If you want to be my people, you must be totally devoted to me.

Gideon had to show whose side he was on. He may have done the deed at night, but everyone soon knew he was on God's side. The idea of being a secret Christian is a ridiculous one. To be a Christian means to be committed to God above everything else — and this should be obvious to everyone who knows you.

GET ON WITH IT

▷ What are you devoted to as much as (or more than) God?

▷ What will you do about this?

▷ Do people around you know you're a Christian?

▷ How should your life reveal your faith more?

PRAY ABOUT IT

Talk through these issues with God, asking Him to help you take a stand for Jesus, being more devoted to Him.

THE BOTTOM LINE

We must all choose sides and wear our team shirts with pride.

➡ TAKE IT FURTHER

Need encouragement? Try page 112.

23 | Give fleece a chance

Not long ago, the Abiezrites had wanted to kill Gideon for trashing their altar to fake god Baal. Now they're going to follow him into battle.

👁 Read Judges 6 v 33–35

ENGAGE YOUR BRAIN

▷ *Who were attacking God's people? (v33)*

▷ *Who were fighting alongside Gideon?*

▷ *But who was behind Gideon and the Israelites? (v34a)*

God gave Gideon His Holy Spirit to supply him with the courage and ability to fight for God. All Christians have God's Spirit in them, giving them the courage and ability to stand up for God.

👁 Read verses 36–40

▷ *What had God promised Gideon? (v36)*

▷ *But what did Gideon want from the Lord? (v37, v39)*

▷ *Incredibly, what did God do? (v38, v40)*

It's as if Gideon's heart was failing him — he knows God's will, but can't bring himself to face it. Maybe the problem isn't that we don't know God's will for us — it's that we don't like it and would rather avoid it. But look at the way God deals with Gideon — tremendous patience, great tenderness. God was going to teach Gideon to trust Him more, but just now Gideon needed reassurance.

GET ON WITH IT

▷ *Is there anything you know God wants you to do but you're trying to avoid it?*

▷ *What will you do about it?*

PRAY ABOUT IT

Praise God for His great kindness and patience despite our reluctance and weakness. Ask Him to give you the courage and ability to do what He wants you to.

→ TAKE IT FURTHER

Further fleece facts — page 112.

24 | God's 300

The Midianite armies are all over the plain like a swarm of locusts, ready to destroy the Israelites. Surely Gideon will need a massive army to fight them. But God has other ideas.

👁 Read Judges 7 v 1–8

▶ *How many men did Gideon start with? (Work it out from v3)*

▶ *How many did God leave him with? (v7)*

▶ *Why? (v2)*

God often uses the weak in His plans. We shouldn't get big-headed when God uses us to serve Him. It's a great privilege to be a part of God's plans, but it doesn't mean we're extra brilliant — it's all down to God.

👁 Read verses 9–15

▶ *How did God encourage Gideon? (v9–11)*

▶ *How large was the enemy army? (v12)*

▶ *What were this powerful army scared of? (v14)*

👁 Read verses 15–25

▶ *What did the 300 men do? (v20)*

▶ *What did God do? (v22)*

There's no mention of Gideon and his men even having weapons with them! This was a stunning victory against a huge enemy, using only trumpets, clay jars and flaming torches. But there was no doubt that it was God's victory. He used this small group of weaponless warriors to defeat a terrifying enemy.

PRAY ABOUT IT

Nothing is impossible for God. No one is more powerful than Him. And He often uses surprising methods and weak people in His perfect plans. None more surprising than Jesus' death to rescue us. Spend time thanking God for these mind-blowing truths about Him.

THE BOTTOM LINE

God wins.

→ TAKE IT FURTHER

More pottery on page 112.

25 Catch some Zs

God had given Gideon and the Israelites an astonishing victory over the Midianites. But the job wasn't finished yet. Gideon was still pursuing the enemy, but some of his own people were getting in the way.

👁 Read Judges 8 v 1–3

ENGAGE YOUR BRAIN

▶ What annoyed the Israelite tribe of Ephraim? (v1)

▶ How would you describe Gideon's reply to them? (v2–3)

The Ephraimites were annoyed that Gideon started the fight without them. They were more interested in grabbing glory for themselves than for God. Gideon could have exploded with anger. Instead, he replied politely and humbly.

GET ON WITH IT

▶ Who really bugs you?

▶ How can you be more humble and gentle with the way you handle them?

👁 Read verses 4–21

▶ How did the people in Succoth and Peniel respond to Gideon's request for help? (v6, v8)

▶ What happened to them? (v16–17)

▶ What had Zebah and Zalmunna done to Gideon's brothers? (v19)

▶ So what happened to Z & Z? (v22)

▶ How did Gideon show his cowardice again? (v20)

The people of Succoth and Peniel didn't trust God to give Gideon the victory so played it safe. But this meant they sided with Israel's enemies and so were punished as Israel's enemies.

THINK ABOUT IT

Ever turn against other Christians? Or get in the way of people serving God? Or cause arguments? Or say stuff behind people's backs? Say sorry to God now for specific times you've done these things.

→ TAKE IT FURTHER

Catch some more advice on p112.

31

26 Not again...

Weak Gideon had become strong because he trusted in God. But it's funny how power often corrupts people. Well, more tragic than funny.

Read Judges 8 v 22–27

ENGAGE YOUR BRAIN
▶ *What did the Israelites get wrong? (v22)*

▶ *What did Gideon get right? (v23)*

▶ *But what did he get badly wrong? (v24–27)*

The Israelites made Gideon their hero, seeming to forget that God was behind all their victories. So Gideon let them know that God was in charge (v23). After saying such a brilliant thing, Gideon messed up big time. He said God should rule Israel but then made a gold ephod (special tunic worn by priests) which people worshipped instead of God! It's easy to say the right, godly thing but then let God down immediately.

Read verses 28–35
▶ *What was the good news? (v28)*

▶ *What was the very bad news? (v33–35)*

Yet again, God's people failed to learn their lesson. They didn't remember all the unbelievable things God had done for them, and they refused to let Him rule them. They went chasing after false gods again. Pathetic.

THINK ABOUT IT
▶ *What things do you worship? What do you make more important than God?*

PRAY ABOUT IT
Talk to God about things you give more time or respect to than Him. Ask Him to help you stop trying to be boss of your own life. If you genuinely mean it, tell God you want Him to be King — in charge of your life.

THE BOTTOM LINE
Put God first in your life.

➔ TAKE IT FURTHER
No *Take it further* today.

27 Trees tease

Gideon (also known as Jerub–Baal) died. He left the Israelites spiralling back into sin and idol worship. He also left 70 sons and a bloodthirsty power struggle.

Read Judges 9 v 1–6

ENGAGE YOUR BRAIN

▶ *Who did the people of Shechem choose as leader?*

▶ *How would you describe him from these verses?*

▶ *What terrible thing did he do? (v5)*

▶ *But who escaped?*

Read verses 7–15

This story has confused people for years. Jotham seems to be accusing the people of choosing a useless thornbush (Abimelech) to be their king, instead of someone good and godly. He makes himself a little clearer in the next section.

Read verses 16–21

▶ *What had Gideon/Jerub-Baal done for the people? (v17)*

▶ *But how had they treated his family? (v18)*

▶ *What would happen to them because of their actions? (v20)*

Despite his confusing tree tale, Jotham is talking sense. God's people should take great care in choosing leaders. And they should treat their leaders (and families) properly.

THINK ABOUT IT

▶ *Are you careful about who you follow and listen to?*

▶ *What are the qualities of a good Christian leader?*

▶ *And a bad one?*

▶ *How well do you treat Christian leaders you know?*

▶ *How will you treat them better?*

PRAY ABOUT IT

Thank God for the people who lead your church / youth group. Ask Him to help you be wise in who you listen to and let influence you.

THE BOTTOM LINE

Follow good, godly leaders.

→ TAKE IT FURTHER

Follow the leader to page 113.

28 Abimelech abolished

Gideon's (Jerub-Baal's) son, Abimelech, killed all his brothers except one. Jotham escaped and told Abimelech and the people of Shechem that, because of their treachery, they'd destroy each other.

Read Judges 9 v 22–25

ENGAGE YOUR BRAIN

▶ How did the people in Shechem treat Abimelech? (v25)

▶ Why? (v23–24)

Read verses 26–41

▶ What did Gaal want? (v29)

▶ What did Zebul do? (v30–33)

▶ What was the outcome? (v39–41)

Read verses 42–57

▶ What did Abimelech's army do to Shechem? (v45)

▶ What else? (v49)

▶ How did Abimelech meet his end? (v53)

▶ Why did all of this happen? (v56–57)

These weren't merely two groups of evil people destroying each other. God was behind it all (v23–24, v56–57). The people of Shechem had foolishly chosen an ungodly leader and had worshipped idols. Abimelech had murdered his own brothers in his hideous pursuit of power. So God punished them by letting them destroy each other.

Sometimes it seems as if evil rules the world. So many horrible things on the news. But God is still in control. His plans are still working out. In the end, God gets the victory. He sent Jesus to win the battle against evil once and for all. Never forget that.

PRAY ABOUT IT

Thank God He's in control and always acts for the good of His people. Pray that you will trust Him more.

THE BOTTOM LINE

God is the perfect judge.

→ TAKE IT FURTHER

More about all this on page 113.

29 Psalms: Soul mate

Time for a musical interlude for a few days, as David sings to God. In this psalm, David's on the run from his son Absalom, who was staging a military coup against his dad. He wanted to be king in David's place.

👁 **Read Psalm 63 v 1–8**

ENGAGE YOUR BRAIN

🔽 What did David thirst for in the desert? (v1)

🔽 How did he describe God's love? (v3)

🔽 How does David respond to it? (v4)

🔽 What is he certain of, even in the harsh desert? (v5)

🔽 What does he hold on to? (v6–8)

Amazing. David is on the verge of losing his kingdom; his son is trying to murder him; yet he doesn't feel sorry for himself. He finds comfort in his God, who he knows loves him and will look after him.

🔽 Could you honestly say that God's love is better than life to you?

👁 **Read verses 9–11**

🔽 What would happen to David's pursuers?

🔽 How could David be so confident?

It's so easy to wallow in self-pity when the world seems to be against us. But David had complete confidence in God to rescue him and deal fairly with his enemies.

THINK ABOUT IT

Go through this psalm verse by verse, looking at David's attitudes to God and to hard times. How do they challenge you in the way you think and act?

PRAY ABOUT IT

Ask God to give you love for Him like David's.

THE BOTTOM LINE

Trust God even in the dark times.

➔ **TAKE IT FURTHER**

More on page 113.

30 | Words and swords

"Go on, you'll get away with it!"
"Who's going to know it was you?"
"Even if you're found out, who cares?"
Ever dished out advice like this? Or been given it?

👁 Read Psalm 64 v 1–6

ENGAGE YOUR BRAIN

▷ *What did David do when he feared for his life? (v1–2)*
▷ *How does he describe hurtful words in v3?*
▷ *What's the answer to the question in v5?*
▷ *What do these people think of themselves? (v6)*

👁 Read verses 7–10

▷ *What shock was in store for these cunning plotters? (v7)*
▷ *What will God do with their nasty words? (v8)*
▷ *When God acts, what's the only response? (v9)*
▷ *What 3 things should believers do? (v10)*

It's just not true that we can get away with stuff. We may fool ourselves that harsh words don't matter if they're behind someone else's back. Or that it's OK to do wrong if no one finds out. But nothing gets past God. Our words often come back to haunt us.

And when people plot against us or hurt us with sharp, vicious words, we should follow David's example. He turned to God for security. He didn't take matters into his own hands or engage in a war of words. David trusted God to protect him, knowing that God always punishes evil in the end. That's why we can feel safe as God's children and should be happy about it! (v10)

THINK ABOUT IT

▷ *What "secret sins" do you have?*
▷ *Who receives most of your harsh words?*
▷ *Who attacks you verbally?*

PRAY ABOUT IT

You know exactly what to talk to God about today.

TAKE IT FURTHER

Verbal proverbs on page 113.

31 | Thanks, God!

Thanksgiving Day is a big thing in the USA — though how many people actually thank God for what He's given them? In the UK, Australia and elsewhere, we don't really celebrate harvest time much. But King David did.

👁 Read Psalm 65 v 1–4

ENGAGE YOUR BRAIN

A few hints: *In Zion* is a way of saying "among God's people". *Atoned* = "paid the price for". *Transgressions* = "sin against God". The temple was a sign of God's presence with His people.

▶ *What big fact about God is David celebrating? (v3–4)*
▶ *How should this make God's people respond? (v1)*

God forgives! Incredible when you see the state we've got ourselves into.

👁 Read verses 5–8

▶ *What do these verses tell us about God?*

Almighty, all-powerful God, who created the world and rules it (v7), rescues His people (v5). The Bible is full of His mighty acts, but even more packed with rescue stories — the ultimate rescue being through Jesus.

👁 Read verses 9–13

▶ *What does David thank God for in these verses?*
▶ *How involved is God in the harvest?*
▶ *Which verses show God's generosity?*

It's really easy to stuff our faces with fantastic food and forget that God provides it for us in a remarkable way. His generosity seems even more amazing when we remember how we've treated Him.

PRAY ABOUT IT

Take your time reading through the psalm again, stopping to praise and thank God along the way.

THE BOTTOM LINE

God forgives, rescues, rules and provides. Now that's worth singing about, isn't it?

➡ TAKE IT FURTHER

No *Take it further* today.

32 | Shout!

What has God done for you? Does He blow your mind sometimes? So do you sing His praises and let everyone know, shouting it from the rooftops? If not, why not?

Read Psalm 66 v 1–7

ENGAGE YOUR BRAIN
▷ *What's the command here? (v2–3)*

▷ *Who should join in? (v1, v4)*

▷ *Why? (v5–7)*

The whole earth should praise God because what He's done for His people has worldwide significance. He rescued the Israelites from Egypt (v6), but He rules over all nations (v7) and sent His Son to rescue anyone who turns to Him for forgiveness.

Read verses 8–15
▷ *What had God done for His people? (v8–9)*

▷ *But what else had He allowed to happen? (v10–11)*

▷ *But what did this lead to? (v12)*

All Christians can thank God for saving them. But do we praise Him so much when life is tough? We should. God uses such times to test us and strengthen us. And we know that in the end He will give us more than we could dream of. In eternity.

Read verses 16–20
▷ *What had God done for this guy? (v19–20)*

▷ *So what did he do about it? (v16)*

GET ON WITH IT
▷ *In 3 minutes, write down as many things as you can think of that God has done for you.*

▷ *Now don't keep them to yourself; think which of those things you will share with people you know.*

▷ *Who will you start with?*

THE BOTTOM LINE
God's so good to you. Shout it out!

TAKE IT FURTHER
Stuff from 2 Kings on page 113.

33 | Small but tasty

Now for a psalm with just seven verses. And two of them are the same. Should be quick and easy. But don't make the mistake of knocking back this psalm without thinking, and failing to taste it. Chew it over.

👁 **Read Psalm 67**

ENGAGE YOUR BRAIN

ᴅ *What's the psalm writer praying about?*

ᴅ *Is there a verse which sums it up?*

ᴅ *What does the psalm tell us about God?*

ᴅ *What's it say about His people?*

ᴅ *What's it say about His world?*

ᴅ *Which verse particularly hits you, and why?*

There's more in this psalm than initially meets the eye. Verse 1 quotes the first words of a prayer that was said for the Israelites (Numbers 6 v 22–27). It's picture language, and it's beautiful. Think what it would mean for God's people to have God's face "shine" upon them.

ᴅ *If that happened, what would would follow? (v2 hints at it)*

God's people would reflect God to the world and make His rescue plan known to everyone.

ᴅ *Then what would happen? (v3–5, v6–7)*

God chose a people for Himself (the Israelites) in order to make Himself known to the whole world. He did this through Jesus — God's blessing to the world. And we point people to Jesus. Through His people, God reaches those who don't know Him.

PRAY ABOUT IT

Use verses 1–2 to help you pray about spreading God's message to others.

THE BOTTOM LINE

God's message is for the whole world.

→ TAKE IT FURTHER

World view on page 114.

Jesus – God or man?

In *Essential*, we take time out to explore key truths about God, the Bible and Christianity. This issue, we look at exactly what the Bible says about Jesus being God.

JESUS IS GOD

No one doubts that Jesus existed — there's too much evidence. Few people doubt He was an inspiring teacher, a fantastic role-model and an amazing leader. But people often ask if He was anything more than that… Should He be remembered as just a good man or viewed in a very different light? In *Essential* in the last issue we saw that Jesus is human. In this issue we look at the fact that He is not merely human — He's God too!

It's a pretty extreme claim to say that a man who walked on earth 2000 years ago is actually God. But if we turn to the Bible we can see that there is tons of evidence:

JESUS SHARES GOD'S NAME

Long before Jesus was born, a prophet promised that one day God would come to earth as a child. He said there would be a baby called:

"Wonderful Counsellor, Mighty God" (Isaiah 9 v 6). Jesus was that baby. His mum was a human being but His Father was God (Luke 1 v 35), which is how He can be both God and man at the same time.

When Jesus was born, angels announced that the Lord (God) had arrived on earth (Luke 2 v 11). As He grew up, He made some shocking claims. He said that He had met Abraham (who lived thousands of years earlier!) and was able to do that because He is the *"I am"* (one of the great Old Testament names for God). And when Jesus was being tried before a Jewish court, He publicly stated that He is the Son of God (Matthew 26 v 63–64).

GOD AND MAN

Over time, His friends gradually came to realize that Jesus was someone special. Even His friend Thomas —

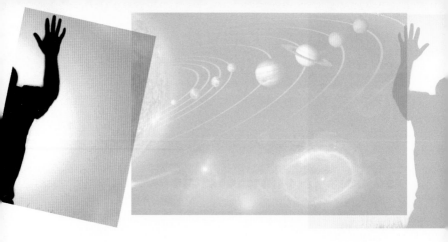

who was a real cynic — ended up calling Jesus: *"My Lord and my God"* (John 20 v 28). The early Christians were equally convinced that Jesus is God. At the start of the Gospel of John, Jesus is referred to as God's "Word" who existed before the beginning of time (John 1 v 1–2). Paul describes Him as *"our great God"* (Titus 2 v 13). And in Revelation, He's described as *"King of kings and Lord of lords"* (Revelation 19 v 16).

So why were all these people convinced that Jesus is God?

JESUS SHOWS GOD'S NATURE

The writer of Hebrews says Jesus is the *"exact representation"* of God (Hebrews 1 v 3) — if we look at Jesus, we see God!

The Bible tells us that Jesus knows everything (John 21 v 17), including people's thoughts (Mark 2 v 8), and is always around (Matthew 28 v 20). In the Gospels we see that Jesus has power over evil (Mark 1 v 27), sickness (Mark 1 v 32–34), nature (Mark 4 v 39) and even death (Mark 5 v 35–42). He even has the power to forgive sins (Mark 2 v 9–12).

And Jesus didn't just die a regular death — He chose to lay down His life and was able to give Himself His life back (John 10 v 17–18). In fact, the Bible even describes Jesus as indestructible (Hebrews 7 v 16) and everlasting (Revelation 22 v 13). These aren't human things — they are God things. Jesus shows that He is God every step of the way.

JESUS DESERVES OUR WORSHIP

All this means that Jesus is not just a person to respect and follow, He is our awesome God. As He entered Jerusalem just before His arrest, the children along the road praised Him and Jesus said it was right for them to do that (Matthew 21 v 16). Jesus invites us to see Him as He really is too — more than a man, the rescuer-God, who can be completely trusted and deserves to be King of our lives.

41

Acts

To be continued...

To Be Continued... How do those words make you feel? Excited? Exasperated? Eager to see what happens next or annoyed by a cop-out cliffhanger? Well, Acts is all about "to be continued".

So far in chapers 1–8 of Acts, we've seen *"all Jesus began to do and to teach"* continuing, with the exciting birth of the church at Pentecost and its growth mainly in Jerusalem and Judea and Samaria. But what about the *"ends of the earth"* where Jesus also sent them (Acts 1 v 8).

Chapters 9 and 10 mark a turning point in the mission of the early church. Firstly, we see a major persecutor of Christians become a believer who's sent out spreading the news. Secondly, we see God's ground-breaking revelation to Peter that the Gentiles, far from being "unclean", could now be part of God's new people.

By the end of the book, the Christian message had reached the heart of the then-known world, Rome itself, and as we leave Paul, we get that "to be continued" feeling again!

Of course, in the centuries that followed Acts, the gospel continued to be preached across the world, until it reached you, wherever you live!

God's mission is still active today, as there are still people and sadly, whole countries, who haven't heard about Jesus' death and resurrection, and the forgiveness and eternal life He offers. But God is still working! His Spirit works in us to get His message out there. Yes, that includes you.

To be continued...

34 | Transformer

Today's section is one of the most famous moments in the book of Acts, and another example of God's transforming power. Remember Saul? It features Saul, who had helped imprison, torture and even kill Christians.

◉ Read Acts 9 v 1–19

ENGAGE YOUR BRAIN

▶ *Sum up Saul's attitude and behaviour towards Christians in v1–2. (The Way = Christianity)*

▶ *How does Jesus describe his behaviour? (v4–5)*

Notice the way Jesus identifies Himself with His people. It's Him Saul is persecuting — not just Christians.

PRAY ABOUT IT

Pray for Christians who are suffering persecution right now. Pray that they'd know the wonderful strength and comfort of being united to Jesus even while suffering.

▶ *What is Ananias' initial reaction to God's command? (v10–14)*

▶ *What is God's answer?*

In case you're wondering, v16 came true. Read 2 Corinthians 11 v 24–29 to see how Saul/Paul suffered for Jesus' name.

▶ *What's so amazing about Ananias' first words to Saul, considering Saul's past?*

The good news about Jesus turns enemies into brothers, makes the blind see and transforms persecutors into believers!

PRAY ABOUT IT

Thank God that although you were once His enemy, Jesus' death and resurrection have made it possible for you to be His friend.

THE BOTTOM LINE

The gospel transforms God's enemies into His friends.

→ TAKE IT FURTHER

Follow the light to page 114.

35 ¦ Go, Saul, go!

Saul's transformation has immediate effects — joy and excitement, along with spreading the message and the persecution that comes with it.

👁 Read Acts 9 v 19–31

ENGAGE YOUR BRAIN

▷ *What is Saul's immediate reaction to God's grace? (v20)*

▷ *What does he preach about Jesus? (v20 and v22)*

▷ *Does God's grace have the same effect on you?*

GET ON WITH IT

A wise man once said that the reason we don't tell others the good news about Jesus, is because either we don't really believe it or we don't care about them. If we've received the gift of God's amazing grace, surely we'll want to share it?

▷ *How do the Jews in Damascus (and Jerusalem) react to Saul's transformation? (v23 and v29)*

▷ *Why is this not surprising? (Acts 9 v 15–16, Luke 9 v 21–23, John 15 v 18–20)*

▷ *What's the reaction of the church in Jerusalem to Saul? (v26)*

But, as in Damascus, fearful former enemies soon become brothers who care for and protect Saul (v27–28).

PRAY ABOUT IT

Think about your church, CU or youth group. The relationships that exist not because of similar interests but only because of a shared love for Jesus are a wonderful sign of God's grace and power. Thank Him for them.

THE BOTTOM LINE

God grows His church in times of both peace and persecution.

→ TAKE IT FURTHER

God and government on page 114.

36 Saints and sinners

Luke wrote Acts. In the first verse of Acts, he talks about his first book (Gospel of Luke), which was about "all that Jesus BEGAN to do and teach". The book of Acts simply carries on the story of Jesus' actions through His church.

◉ Read Acts 9 v 32–43

ENGAGE YOUR BRAIN

▶ How are the believers described in v32? Do you think of yourself that way?

The great thing about being a Christian is that God counts us as washed clean of our sins by Jesus' blood. Our status is one of "saints", God's holy people. Not because of our "saintly" deeds, but because of the cosmic swap that took place on the cross; our sins for Christ's righteousness!

PRAY ABOUT IT

Thank God for that wonderful truth now! Ask Him to help you to live up to your calling — to be what you are.

▶ What miraculous act does Peter perform in v34?
▶ In whose name / under whose authority?
▶ Can you think of any similar miracle performed by Jesus? (eg.

Luke 5 v 18–26)
▶ What miraculous act does Peter perform in v36–40?
▶ Remind you of anything? (eg. Luke 8 v 49–56)

Jesus may have left the disciples but His Spirit is still with them, working through them. We may not have healed anyone or raised anyone from the dead personally, but it's no less true that God's Spirit is with us today if we are Christians.

TALK IT OVER

Chat with an older Christian about what it means to have the Holy Spirit in our lives. Good Bible bits to start your discussion are Romans 15 v 13, 1 Corinthians chs 12–14, Galatians 5 v 22–23.

THE BOTTOM LINE

Jesus is still at work today.

→ TAKE IT FURTHER

More about Dorcas on page 114.

37 Belly vision

A major shift is about to take place. With a few exceptions, the gospel (the good news about Jesus) has only been shared with the Jews, God's historic chosen people. But all that is about to change!

Read Acts 10 v 1–8

ENGAGE YOUR BRAIN
▶ Who are the main characters in this section?

▶ What do we know about each of them?

Read verses 9–23

▶ What is the issue Peter faces in this vision?

▶ As Peter ponders the meaning of the vision, how does God provide the answer? (v17)

In the Old Testament, God commanded His people to be separate from the nations around them. One way this was displayed was in what they did and didn't eat — what was clean and unclean. By New Testament times this, extended to seeing non-Jewish people as unclean too. In Peter's vision, God was saying those boundaries no longer existed.

TALK IT OVER
We may not go so far as to call non-Christians "unclean", but do we still have distinctions and prejudices in our heads. Do we really believe that the gospel is for all people? The Muslim, the Sikh, the Hindu? The atheist? The rapist, the paedophile or the murderer?

PRAY ABOUT IT
Pray about all the people you come into contact with. Are there any you probably wouldn't share the gospel with? Ask for God's forgiveness now and ask Him to give you a love for them and opportunities to share Jesus with them.

THE BOTTOM LINE
God breaks down boundaries.

→ TAKE IT FURTHER
Be gentle to Gentiles — page 114.

38 | No favourites

Things are defrosting between Peter and the Gentiles. He's invited them to be his guests (he's already staying with a tanner who deals with unclean animal skins) so things are thawing nicely. What will happen next?

👁 **Read Acts 10 v 23–35**

ENGAGE YOUR BRAIN

▷ *How eager was Cornelius to hear from Peter? (See his preparations in v24.)*

PRAY ABOUT IT

It's great when people are so eager to hear about Jesus that they invite their friends along to hear too! Pray for any outreach events your church or youth group might be planning — that people would be eager to come along and listen, and that they'd bring their friends too.

▷ *What mistake does Cornelius make at first? (v25)*

▷ *How has God been at work behind the scenes of this historic meeting? (See v28, v31, v33)*

▷ *Has Peter understood what God is doing now? (v28)*

▷ *How do his actions show that?*

▷ *In what way does God not show favouritism? (v34–35)*

Despite all of Cornelius' prayers and gifts to the poor, he still needs Jesus. It's not until he hears the gospel message that Peter is about to share with him that he receives the Holy Spirit and becomes part of God's family.

SHARE IT

Often we find that some non-Christians are nicer, kinder and seem more "Christian" than we are. But it's not being good that saves you — it's being forgiven. Can you share that surprising truth with someone today?

THE BOTTOM LINE

God doesn't show favouritism.

➔ **TAKE IT FURTHER**

More stuff about stuff on page 115.

39 | Crunch time

After all this build up, we finally hear the message. How will Cornelius and co react? After all God has done so far, it's going to be pretty important...

👁 Read Acts 10 v 34–48

ENGAGE YOUR BRAIN

▶ *How does Peter explain the good news about Jesus to Cornelius (v34–43)? Jot down his key points:*

•

•

•

•

•

•

SHARE IT

Could you use Peter's summary to help you explain the gospel? Practise it in your own words and pray for an opportunity to share it this week.

▶ *How do Cornelius and his family and friends respond?*

▶ *How amazing is this turn of events? (See Peter's companions' reaction in v45)*

PRAY ABOUT IT

Thank God for saving Cornelius' family and friends, and pray that He might show the same grace and mercy to people you know. Pray for them by name. Remember Jesus is Lord of all, He is Judge of all, and everyone who believes in Him receives forgiveness of sins.

THE BOTTOM LINE

Jesus is Lord of all.

➔ TAKE IT FURTHER

No *Take it further* today, so you've got extra time to practise explaining the gospel.

40 | Suspicious minds

After the exciting events of chapter 10 you might have expected the church in Jerusalem to be buzzing. Hmmm, not quite.

👁 Read Acts 11 v 1–18

ENGAGE YOUR BRAIN

▷ *What is the issue the circumcised believers have? (v2–3)*

▷ *Is their criticism fair?*

▷ *How does Peter defend himself/ God? (v5, v9, v12, v13, v15, v17)*

▷ *What is his key point? (v17)*

▷ *How do the circumcised believers then respond? (v18)*

God doesn't necessarily always do things the way we expect or want. Initially, the Jews were privileged to be God's chosen people. But now God is including all people in His offer of *"repentance unto life"*. Of course this is nothing new, but maybe these Jews had forgotten Genesis 12 v 3.

PRAY ABOUT IT

Thank God that from the beginning He planned that all peoples on earth would be blessed through Abraham and his descendant Jesus. Pray for countries where there is no strong Christian presence — that the good news about Jesus would reach people there.

SHARE IT

Do you sometimes forget that saving people is God's work? He will do all He has said He'll do and He can save anyone. We don't have to have all the answers, but amazingly God does use us to get His message out. Ask Him now to help you talk about Jesus to someone this week and ask Him to be at work in them.

➡ TAKE IT FURTHER

Don't be suspicious; turn to p115.

41 | Ready steady grow

If you've got a new plant, how do you encourage it to grow? What would you do for it? And what about a new church? How would you encourage that to grow?

Read Acts 11 v 19–30

ENGAGE YOUR BRAIN

- What's the unexpected effect of persecuting the early church? (v19–21)
- Who gets to hear the message? (v19–20)
- Is this part of God's plan? (v21)

Despite the lesson they'd learned from Peter's encounter with Cornelius, the church in Jerusalem is still wary of these Gentile Christians, so they send Barnabas to check out what's going on. Barnabas' name means *"son of encouragement"*.

- What's Barnabas' reaction? (v23)

PRAY ABOUT IT

See how Barnabas is described in v24. Wouldn't you love to be described that way? Pray that God would help you to see the good in situations rather than always being critical. Pray that God would help you to love and encourage other believers.

- What does Barnabas do to encourage the church at Antioch to grow? (v25–26)
- What happened between the Jewish believers and Gentile Christians? (v27–30)

This breaking down of boundaries wasn't just a one-way thing. Bitter enemies become brothers. We've seen it with Saul and now between Jews and Gentiles.

GET ON WITH IT

What can you do to love and encourage other Christians today? A word, an email, a text? Turning up to a Christian meeting to encourage others? Will you love the whole family of believers, not just the ones you'd naturally get on with?

THE BOTTOM LINE

Faith brings with it a family.

→ TAKE IT FURTHER

Grow for it... page 115.

42 | Peter, prayer & persecution

After the gospel explosion of chapter 11, was everything now nice and cosy, sweet and rosy? Nope. Persecution of Christians became very popular. Only this time you'd pay for being a Christian with your life.

👁 Read Acts 12 v 1–19

ENGAGE YOUR BRAIN

▶ *What does Herod do and why? (v1–3)*

▶ *What does he try to do next? (v4)*

▶ *How does the church respond? (v5, v12)*

You might remember that Jesus had warned James and his brother John they would *"drink the same cup"* that Jesus did, and sure enough James goes on to face execution like his master. Remember too what Jesus told Peter about his future? (See John 21 v 18–19 for a reminder.)

TALK IT OVER

Jesus told His followers that if they wanted to be His disciples, they should take up their cross and follow Him. For most of us, being a Christian won't mean dying for our faith. But for lots of people today it does, and one day it might for you. Have you faced that truth? Chat and pray it over with another Christian.

▶ *What does Peter initially think is going on when the angel shows up? (v9)*

▶ *What does he eventually realise God has done? (v11)*

Things look pretty hopeless in v1 — a godless king threatening God's people. But God is the true King, as His rescue of Peter demonstrates. More on this in the next study.

▶ *Despite all their prayers, how do the believers respond to Peter's appearance? (v14–16)*

▶ *How does Herod react? (v19)*

PRAY ABOUT IT

Prayer changes things. God can and will act. Will you let that affect how you pray now?

THE BOTTOM LINE

The Christian life = suffering and then glory.

→ TAKE IT FURTHER

Dying for more? Try page 115.

43 | Herod humbled

King Herod is still throwing his weight around in these next few verses. But he's forgotten who the real King is...

👁 Read Acts 12 v 19–24

ENGAGE YOUR BRAIN

▶ How important do you think Herod felt on his diplomatic visit? (v19–21)

▶ List the things that might have made him feel this way.

▶ How do the people flatter him? (v22)

▶ How does God respond to this nonsense? (v23)

▶ What is the stark contrast in v23–24?

▶ What did Herod set out to do in the early verses of chapter 12?

▶ Did he succeed?

GET ON WITH IT

Are you ever tempted to think too highly of yourself? Read what the apostle Paul said of himself in

1 Timothy 1 v 12–16. As Christians we can relate to his words if we've ever thought honestly about our own sin. Do you need to correct the way you think about yourself today?

PRAY ABOUT IT

Thank God that His plans for the gospel message to spread are unstoppable. Pray for that message to spread in your school, college, workplace, community, town, country and world!

THE BOTTOM LINE

God is the King!

→ TAKE IT FURTHER

A little bit more on page 115.

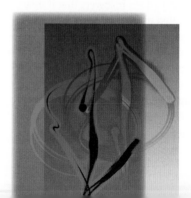

Lamentations

Down but not out

Hearing someone cry — really sob their hearts out — can be an unnerving experience. Welcome to Lamentations. No room for jokes here. It's a book of laments and mourning. A book of deep-seated guilt and sadness.

DEVASTATED CITY

The time and place is 587 BC in Jerusalem. The city had been besieged, ransacked and destroyed by an army from Babylon. What's left was stomach-churning: a city knocked down, its temple invaded, homes wrecked, families broken, corpses left unburied, children's bodies even being used for food.

THE REASON

The sober truth is that the Babylonians had been sent by God Himself. God's people now found God destroying them in anger. But why did God bring such judgment on His own people and on the city where He shared His presence with them?

Well, God's people, who'd repeatedly turned their backs on Him, were being brought to their senses in an unmissable way. After being given many chances to live God's way, they were now being made to realise the true character of the God they'd rejected so many times.

RAY OF HOPE

But even in the middle of God's punishment, there remained the possibility of a way out of this despair. There are little rays of hope poking out of the dark in Lamentations. And if you look closely, you'll see they've got "Jesus" written all over them.

God's people were seriously down. But not out. It wasn't entirely over between God and His people. There really could be hope. And we'll see why as we look into this often-avoided book.

44 | Jerusalem judged

Lamentations is a book to read out loud. To perform. Go on, try reading chapter one with some of the wrenching emotion it's written with.

👁 Read Lamentations 1 v 7

ENGAGE YOUR BRAIN

▷ How is the past of Jerusalem described? (v1, v7)

▷ What was it like now? (v6–7)

▷ What happened to God's people? (v3, v5)

👁 Read verses 8–17

▷ Why was Jerusalem in this depressing state? (v12–13)

▷ Why did God punish His people? (v8, v14)

Jerusalem was besieged and devastated. Its heart, the temple, invaded. Its people slaughtered, others captured. No food to survive on. And it was all God's doing. And rightly so. They had rejected God again and again, not listening to His warnings. So God allowed their enemies to destroy Jerusalem.

👁 Read verses 18–22

▷ What did the people of Jerusalem recognise? (v18a, v20)

▷ But what did they want God to do? (v21–22)

This chapter presents a gloomy picture of a city under God's judgment. A people who hadn't given a thought to what their persistent wrongdoing would lead to. Until it was too late.

THINK ABOUT IT

▷ How does this chapter change your view of God?
▷ How should you behave differently?

PRAY ABOUT IT

Ask God for the wisdom to view sin as seriously as He does.

→ TAKE IT FURTHER

More background on page 115.

45 | Consequences of sin

In Lamentations, Jerusalem's often called "Daughter of Zion". It's a way of saying these guys were God's chosen people. So the first verse we read today is a bit of a shocker.

👁 Read Lamentations 2 v 1–9

Imagine you're a Jew, living in Jerusalem. You believed God would look after you, one of His privileged people. Find all the actions in v1–9 which would be completely horrifying to you. And think why.

Read verses 10–17

ENGAGE YOUR BRAIN

▷ *How did the city's leaders feel about what was happening? (v10)*

▷ *What had gone wrong? (v14)*

▷ *How would listening to God have helped His people? (v17)*

The prophet's job was to call God's people back to His covenant — His promise to give them a great life as they obeyed His laws. But, over centuries, they'd ignored their duty to God, listened to false prophets, and were now receiving the consequences. Just as God had also promised.

👁 Read verses 18–22

▷ *What depths have God's people sunk to? (v20)*

▷ *What does the writer desperately want the people to do? (v18–19)*

God's people chose to ignore repeated warnings that their sin would bring God's punishment. They were totally mistaken. God always keeps His word (v17).

PRAY ABOUT IT

Thank God that even though we fully deserve His anger, He doesn't act uncontrollably and He always keeps His word. Thank Him that even though we deserve destruction, He sent His Son to rescue us.

THE BOTTOM LINE

God always keeps His word.

→ TAKE IT FURTHER

Warning: don't miss page 115.

46 Good grief

Fed up with Lamentations yet? It seems to be a never-ending poem of misery. Well, chapter 3 continues on the same note. But hang in there, hope can be found in the darkness...

👁 Read Lamentations 3 v 1–18

ENGAGE YOUR BRAIN

▶ How would you sum up these verses in one sentence?

▶ Who is the "He" who has caused all this suffering?

Jerusalem has suffered greatly at the hands of the Babylonians. But God is behind it all, punishing His people for turning away from Him and sinning hideously. Amazingly, it's not all bad news...

👁 Read verses 19–30

▶ What's the big change from v19–20 to v21?

▶ What caused it? (v22–24)

▶ Even though God has punished His people, what do they know about Him? (v25)

▶ So what should they do? (v26–28)

👁 Read verses 31–39

▶ Does God enjoy punishing people? (v33)

▶ Do people have any reason to complain about God's judgment? (v39)

▶ What's the great hope for God's people? (v31–32)

Lamentations is a dark book. But here we see the hope that believers hold on to: God's compassion never fails; He is completely faithful; His people will inherit eternal life with Him (v24 hints at this); God is good to those whose hope is in Him; He will save them. That's why He sent Jesus.

PRAY ABOUT IT

Turn verses 19–32 into a prayer or song of praise and thanks to our glorious God.

THE BOTTOM LINE

God punishes sin, but He shows unfailing compassion to His people.

→ TAKE IT FURTHER

More encouragement on page 116.

47 | Aggressive prayer

How do you feel when people mess you around and treat you really badly? The writer of Lamentations isn't exactly subtle as he cries out to God for vengeance. But first, a few positive words.

◉ Read Lam 3 v 40–42

ENGAGE YOUR BRAIN

▷ How should God's people respond to Him?

▷ When did you last take a long look at your actions and habits and admit your sin to God?

PRAY ABOUT IT
Don't delay. Do it right now.

◉ Read verses 43–54

▷ How were God's people viewed by other nations? (v45–47)

▷ But what was worse? (v43–44)

▷ What was their only hope? (v49–50)

It's a terrible thing to live without God's forgiveness, under His judgment, with your prayers unheard. But that's not the end of the story for God's people.

◉ Read verses 55–66

▷ What's the big encouragement? (v55–58)

▷ So what did the writer pray for his enemies? (v64–66)

In the middle of these gloomy words, there's encouragement — God won't turn away from those who admit their sin and ask for forgiveness.

Nevertheless, this guy's response seems a bit over the top. But he knows how much God hates sin and must punish those who oppose Him. And instead of taking matters into his own hands, he asks God to deal with them. Leave judgment to God, the perfect Judge.

PRAY ABOUT IT
Talk to God honestly about what's on your mind now. It might be suffering, sin struggles, friends who reject God's forgiveness, or people who seem to get away with wrong. Or something else. God wants to hear and He wants to help.

→ TAKE IT FURTHER
There's no lamenting on page 116.

48 | Wrecked by sin

After yesterday's ray of hope, we walk back into the gloom of life in Jerusalem under God's judgment. See if you can spot the one verse of hope in the whole chapter.

👁 Read Lamentations 4 v 1–16

ENGAGE YOUR BRAIN

▷ *Does gold usually lose its shine?*

▷ *So what's the writer saying about Jerusalem? (v1–2, v5)*

▷ *Why was Jerusalem suffering? (v11, v13)*

These were God's chosen people — the most privileged group of guys there was. Yet they threw it all away and rejected God, who'd done so much for them. And their own prophets and priests had led them away from the Lord. That's why He punished them.

👁 Read verses 17–22

▷ *What mistakes did the people make? (v17, v20)*

▷ *Where should they have been looking for rescue?*

▷ *What hope are they given? (v22)*

▷ *But who is singled out for punishment? (v21–22)*

God's people hadn't trusted in the Lord to lead them and give them peace, security and prosperity. They'd turned from Him and looked to other nations to rescue them. Instead, they were invaded and Jerusalem was destroyed. But God's punishment wouldn't last forever (v22). And their enemies would be judged. Edom (v21–22) stands for all other nations. Anyone who goes against God will one day face His judgment.

PRAY ABOUT IT

Jerusalem's sin made God angry and made life a nightmare. Think about saying sorry to God for the way your sin has offended Him and spoilt life for others around you.

THE BOTTOM LINE

Sin wrecks everything.

→ TAKE IT FURTHER

Never read Obadiah? Go to page 116.

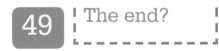

49 | The end?

Had God rejected His people? In His judgment, had He finally abandoned them? Was the relationship over? See what the writer pleaded next.

Read Lamentations 5 v 1–18

ENGAGE YOUR BRAIN

▷ *What was the plea? (v1)*

▷ *How would you sum up the state of Jerusalem (v2–18) in one sentence?*

▷ *Again, what reason is given? (v7, v16)*

Throughout the Old Testament, God had promised to make His people into a great nation, to give them a land and to bless them. But here we see the opposite of that. And they were to blame for this fall from grace.

Read verses 19–22

▷ *What did the writer remember about God? (v19)*

▷ *What did he long for God to do? (v21)*

▷ *But what did he fear? (v20, v22)*

Unlike the people of Jerusalem back then, we know the full story. The New Testament makes it clear that God hasn't forgotten His people and offers them a way back to a close relationship with Him. Jesus took God's punishment in our place, to remove God's anger against us. To repair that broken relationship. And make it unbreakable.

Lamentations presents a desperate picture of God's people. They were down but not out — God's unfailing compassion brings hope through Jesus. So let's go on to lead lives that show our thanks to Him.

PRAY ABOUT IT

What have you learned and been challenged about as you've read Lamentations? Talk with God about what He's said to you through this no-nonsense book.

→ TAKE IT FURTHER

One last lament on page 116.

TOOLBOX

Pray as you learn

One of the main ambitions of **engage** is to encourage you to dive into God's word and learn how to handle it and understand it more. Each issue, TOOLBOX gives you tips, tools and advice for wrestling with the Bible.

In previous Toolbox articles we've been looking at different tools we can use to help us understand and apply what we read in God's word. But after you've read a part of the Bible, how should you respond?

TALKING WITH GOD

You might have heard prayer described as a two-way conversation, where God speaks to us and we speak to God. But the Bible doesn't use the word "prayer" in that way. Prayer is simply when we talk to God. Others think of reading the Bible as a conversation, in which God speaks to us and we bring our own meanings to the passage so that we have a voice too. But that's not really right, either.

We have a conversation when we hear God speak to us through the Bible and then we speak to Him in prayer. There's a vivid description of this happening in Nehemiah chapters 8 and 9. For seven whole days, Ezra the scribe read God's law (part of the Old Testament) to the people. As they heard God speaking to them, the people were deeply moved to sadness and to joy too. There were tears as well as celebration feasts. And in response to what they heard, they poured out their hearts in prayer to God.

So how is it that often when we read the Bible and then pray, our prayers have nothing to do with God's word, which we've just read? We don't take our part in the conversation. We ignore what God has said to us and concentrate mostly on whatever needs and wants are taking over our thoughts right now.

PRAYER DISCIPLINE

Like everything in your spiritual life, prayer doesn't just happen. It takes discipline. A good idea is to keep a daily prayer journal. List all the

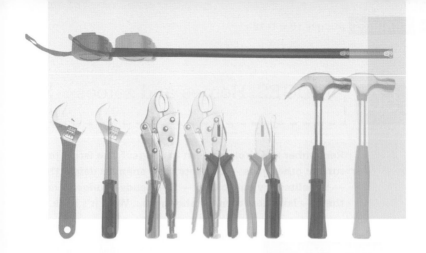

people and things you'll pray about regularly. Also record what you've learned in the Bible. And jot down things you've prayed about and how you've seen prayer answered. And make sure you set aside time every day to talk to God.

It's good to get into the habit of praying about the stuff God's taught you in the Bible. Here are some prayers you can try:

"Sorry for _____, which your word has shown me is wrong in my life."

"Thank you for _____, which amazed me when I read about it."

"Please give me the strength to change _____ in response to what you've been saying to me."

Read Colossians 3 v 1–14

▷ *What motivations are given in these verses to forgive?*

▷ *Think about what the Lord has done for you. How does that change your worldview (your values, priorities, view of yourself and of others)?*

▷ *How will this help you forgive other Christians?*

▷ *What would be an appropriate prayer in the light of what you've learned?*

So go on, pray that prayer!

Ideas taken from Dig Deeper by Nigel Beynon and Andrew Sach. Published by IVP and available from thegoodbook.co.uk

50 | JUDGES: Heroes and zeroes

Remember the circle pattern in Judges? The Israelites turn to other gods — God lets their enemies defeat them — Israelites cry out to God — God sends a judge to rescue them — Israelites turn to other gods... Well, it's back.

👁 Read Judges 10 v 1–5

▷ *What are we told about Tola?*

▷ *And Jair?*

We know virtually nothing about these judges, but they led Israel for 45 years. We're told that Tola *"saved Israel"* after evil Abimelech had tried to destroy it. He's unknown nowadays, but God used him to save His people! All we know about Jair is his 30 sons on 30 donkeys in 30 cities. God chooses all kinds of people to serve Him — famous, unknown, big, small, male, female, shy, confident. That means He can use **you** to serve Him in a big way. Will you let Him?

👁 Read verses 6–16

▷ *Spot the circle pattern again*
  v6:
  v6–8:
  v10:

▷ *But how did God answer the Israelites' cries?*

▷ *How did the Israelites show they really meant it? (v15–16)*

God was fed up with rescuing His people over and over only for them to abandon Him for fake gods. So He said: *"Go to those useless gods for help, I won't save you any more."* God won't tolerate sin and rejection forever. And yet He's still so loving. Verse 16 is amazing: *"He could bear Israel's misery no longer."* God hates to see His people suffer. Even though they'd abandoned Him again and again, He would rescue them once more.

PRAY ABOUT IT

Thank God for His fairness, His hatred of sin and His unbelievable love for His people. Ask Him to help you turn away from false "gods" and live for Him wholeheartedly.

→ TAKE IT FURTHER

Try page 117.

51 ¦ Judge Jephthah

God gave Israel another judge to rescue them. Check out how the Israelites treated Jephthah the same way we saw them treat God yesterday — rejecting him and then turning to him for undeserved help.

👁 **Read Judges 10 v 17–11 v 11**

ENGAGE YOUR BRAIN

▶ What promises did Israel's leaders make? (10 v 18)

▶ Who did they ask to save them from the Ammonites?

▶ Why was this a surprise? (11 v 1–2)

▶ What were they doing right this time? (v10–11)

Another unlikely hero. Jephthah was the son of a prostitute, rejected by his own family and living in exile with a band of adventurers. But God uses the most surprising heroes to save His people. Jesus, too, was despised by many and had to flee His home, but God used Him to bring the ultimate rescue to His people.

Read verses 12–28

▶ Why did the Ammonites attack Israel? (v13)

▶ What 3 answers did Jephthah give to the Ammonites' claims?
v15:
v23:
v26–27:

▶ How did the king respond? (v28)

Even though the Ammonites were being ridiculous with their claims on the land, Jephthah tried hard to make peace with them, rather than go to war immediately. Our first reaction to injustice is often to go on the attack, rather than to try and make peace.

GET ON WITH IT

▶ Who have you fallen out with?
▶ How can you try to sort things out in a peaceful way?

PRAY ABOUT IT

Ask God to help you be calm like Jephthah as you talk to that person. Ask Him to help you make peace.

→ **TAKE IT FURTHER**

More on page 117.

52 | Tragic victory

The Ammonites wanted to kick God's people out of their own country. So the Israelites made Jephthah their leader, hoping he'd rescue them and defeat the Ammonites.

👁 Read Judges 11 v 29–33

ENGAGE YOUR BRAIN

▶ How was Jephthah able to lead the Israelites? (v29)

▶ What had he promised God? (v30–31)

▶ What did God enable Jephthah to do? (v32–33)

God gave His Holy Spirit to help Jephthah (as He does to all believers); Jephthah trusted God and made a serious promise to Him; God gave Israel a huge victory. Sounds great, but this story had a tragic ending.

👁 Read verses 34–40

▶ What shock awaited Jephthah as he arrived home in victory? (v34)

▶ Why was this happy event actually so tragic? (v30–31, v35)

▶ What was brilliant about his daughter's response? (v36)

▶ What was her final request? (v37)

Heartbreaking. God gave Jephthah and the Israelites a great victory over their enemy, but celebration was short-lived. Because of a rash promise Jephthah made, he lost his only daughter. Truly tragic.

THINK ABOUT IT

▶ Do you ever make promises you can't keep?

▶ Ever speak before you think?

▶ Will you think twice before saying stuff that may have a bad effect in the future?

PRAY ABOUT IT

Thank God that He gives Christians His Spirit to help them serve Him. Ask Him to help you think before you speak and not make foolish promises.

→ TAKE IT FURTHER

No Take it further today.

53 ⌐ Give God the glory ¬

God rescued His people from their enemies yet again, with Jephthah leading them to victory. But because of a rash promise, he lost his daughter. And now some fellow Israelites are causing trouble.

👁 **Read Judges 12 v 1–7**

ENGAGE YOUR BRAIN

▶ *What was the problem for the Israelite tribe of Ephraim? (v1)*

▶ *How did Jephthah answer them? (v2–3)*

▶ *Then what did Jephthah and his men do?*

The Ephraimites and the Gileadites were all Israelites — God's people. Yet they attacked each other because of the pride of the Ephraimites. They wanted to be in control; they wanted to get the praise.

THINK ABOUT IT

Do you always want to be the one who's seen to be serving God? Are you prepared to serve God behind the scenes as well as in the limelight? Christians should want God to get the glory, not themselves.

👁 **Read verses 8–15**

▶ *What do we learn about these leaders of Israel?*
Ibzan:

Elon:

Abdon:

Some judges have loads written about them. Others (like Ibzan, Elon and Abdon) are barely mentioned. But it doesn't really matter. The book of Judges is all about God, not these people. It's great that God used these men and women to lead His people. But it was God who rescued them. It's God who is in control. And it's God who should get all the praise from His people!

PRAY ABOUT IT

Spend time thanking and praising God for who He is. And for what He's done for His people by sending Jesus to rescue them.

→ **TAKE IT FURTHER**

Spot the difference on page 117.

54 | Angel delight

Yet again the Israelites turned away from God. This time He punished them by letting the Philistines rule them oppressively for a whopping 40 years. But God is going to give His people another rescuer.

👁 Read Judges 13 v 1–5

ENGAGE YOUR BRAIN

- ▶ What was the bad news for Manoah and his wife? (v2)
- ▶ What surprising news did God's angel bring? (v3)
- ▶ What specific instructions did she have to follow? (v4–5)
- ▶ What would be special about this baby boy? (v5)

Yet again, God used someone surprising in His plans. This time it was Manoah and his wife (who was unable to have kids). But the angel of the Lord had news for her, as well as a programme to follow before and after the birth of her miracle baby. We don't even know this woman's name, but God included her in His rescue plans. So never think you're too insignificant for God.

This baby was not allowed to have his hair cut. It was a sign that he was special — set apart to serve God. He would begin to rescue Israel from the Philistines (v5). This baby would grow up to be a saviour of God's people, but he'd only begin the job. David would complete the rescue from the Philistines.

This boy, Samson, is only a partial saviour, but he points us to the perfect Saviour — Jesus Christ. Jesus finished the job for good. By His death and resurrection, Jesus offers complete rescue from sin and death.

PRAY ABOUT IT

Ask God to give you the confidence and ability to serve Him, even if you don't understand why He'd ever use you in His plans. Thank Him for sending Jesus, the perfect Saviour, who offers rescue to anyone who trusts in Him.

THE BOTTOM LINE

Samson began to save, Jesus saves completely.

→ TAKE IT FURTHER

Dare to be different on page 117.

55 | Flame and fortune

The angel of the Lord visited Manoah's wife and told her she would miraculously have a baby who she must set apart to serve God. When Manoah heard about it, he wanted to know more.

👁 **Read Judges 13 v 6–18**

ENGAGE YOUR BRAIN

▶ What did Manoah ask God? (v8)

▶ What did the angel tell him? (v13–14)

▶ How much of this was new info?

▶ What had Manoah not yet understood? (v16–18)

The angel of the Lord speaks God's exact words. They are with God Himself. But they've not realised that yet. They think He's just a messenger.

Manoah wanted more instructions about how to bring up their son. But the angel merely repeated the original orders. Sometimes we want to know more from God, but what we really need to hear is what He's already told us. There's no point asking God for more if we're not obeying what He's already taught us.

👁 **Read verses 19–25**

▶ What amazing thing happened?

▶ How did Manoah react? (v22)

▶ But what did his wife know? (v23)

▶ What was the happy outcome? (v24–25)

Manoah realised how awesome and powerful God is. He didn't think he could survive being in God's presence. He was terrified. We rarely give God the respect He deserves. He's awesome, mighty and terrifying.

PRAY ABOUT IT

Thank God that Jesus has made it possible for us to safely approach Him. Ask Him to help you treat Him with the respect and awe He deserves.

→ TAKE IT FURTHER

No *Take it further* today.

56

Roars, riddles and relatives

Baby Samson was chosen to serve God in a special way. The scene now switches to Samson as a young man. Time to fight a lion and find a wife.

👁 Read Judges 14 v 1–7

ENGAGE YOUR BRAIN

▶ What was surprising about Samson's choice of wife? (v2–3)

▶ But what did Samson's parents not realise? (v4)

▶ Where did Samson's devastating strength come from? (v6)

The Philistines were ruling over the Israelites oppressively. God's people were not supposed to marry people from other godless nations. But Samson liked the look of a Philistine girl and God used this in His plans to defeat the Philisitines. Already we can see the Holy Spirit at work in Samson, giving him the power to kill a lion with his bare hands.

👁 Read verses 8–20

▶ What did Samson's bet lead to? (v15–17)

▶ How did Samson get the clothes needed to pay the winners? (v19)

▶ What happened to his bride? (v20)

This isn't the last time we'll see Samson give in to nagging with disastrous consequences. It seems unfair that Samson killed 30 random people for their clothes, but it was all part of God's plan to punish the Philistines and rescue the Israelites from them. Samson and the Philistines now hate each other. Sparks will fly. More tomorrow.

PRAY ABOUT IT

Weird things happen in this chapter, but God is using all of them in His great rescue plan. Thank God that even in the chaos and confusion of life, He is in complete control, putting His big rescue plan into action.

➔ TAKE IT FURTHER

Roaring success — page 118.

57 | Fox tails and donkey jaws

God's plan to rescue His people from the cruel Philistines is under way. Samson has already fallen out with some Philistines, killed some others and lost his wife to one. He's not happy...

👁 **Read Judges 15 v 1–8**

ENGAGE YOUR BRAIN

▶ What provoked Samson's anger against the Philistines? (v1–3)

▶ In what bizarre way did he take revenge? (v4–5)

▶ How did the Philistines retaliate? (v6)

▶ And Samson? (v8)

👁 **Read verses 9–20**

▶ How did the locals react to Samson hiding from the Philistines in their territory? (v11)

▶ How did Samson use the situation to his advantage? (v12–15)

▶ Yet what nearly killed him? (v18)

▶ How did God save him? (v19)

An even bigger shock than Samson using a donkey jaw as a weapon was Judah's cowardice. This Israelite tribe had always been ready to fight God's enemies (see Judges 1 v 1–4), but here they seemed happy to be ruled by the Philistines! But Samson wasn't happy, and God's Spirit gave him the strength to kill 1000 enemies.

Samson knew that God had given him this victory. But the hero who'd killed 1000 enemies was thirsty, weak and near death. So again he had to rely on God to save him. And God miraculously gave Samson the water he needed. If even brave, heroic Samson turned to God for help, then we should do the same. We should rely on Him for the strength to fight against God's enemies — the sin in our lives.

PRAY ABOUT IT

Ask God to give you the strength to serve Him. The strength to fight the sin in your life.

➡ **TAKE IT FURTHER**

Feeling foxed? Turn to page 118.

58 Strength and weakness

As part of His rescue plans, God gave Samson the strength to defeat his enemies. But Samson also had weaknesses.

👁 Read Judges 16 v 1–3

ENGAGE YOUR BRAIN

▶ *What was Samson's weakness? (also 14 v 1 and 16 v 4)*

▶ *What danger did it lead to? (v2)*

▶ *How did he escape? (v3)*

Samson was a Nazirite — someone set aside to serve God with His life. But he wouldn't give his whole life to God. Sex was too big a temptation for him and it got him into trouble. But God didn't take Samson's strength away from him and he showed his power once again (v3). Tomorrow we'll see Samson fall for another woman and get into far worse trouble.

THINK ABOUT IT

▶ *Do you have a weakness for the opposite sex?*

▶ *Do you find sex or porn or sexual temptation too hard to resist?*

▶ *Do you tend to fall for the "wrong sort" — people who don't share your faith?*

"The Philistines were obviously against God, but this non-Christian girl/guy is so nice..." It's too dangerous. So many people are slowly enticed away from their love of Jesus by people who may be lovely but don't love Jesus. If you're a believer, rule out the possibility of a relationship with them. Samson's service of God was wrecked, and the devil can do the same to you.

"But there's no harm in being friends... I won't get too involved... I know when to stop..." Don't kid yourself. Playing with temptation is a very dangerous game — as Samson was going to find to his cost.

PRAY ABOUT IT

Talk to God about anything He's challenged you about today. Be honest with Him. Ask for His help. Then take steps to deal with it.

➔ TAKE IT FURTHER

More sex stuff on page 118.

59 | Hair today, gone tomorrow

Samson was the strongest man around. But his strength came from God. His weakness for the opposite sex would get between him and God and make him as weak as a kitten.

👁 Read Judges 16 v 4–14

ENGAGE YOUR BRAIN

▷ *What persuaded Delilah to betray Samson? (v5)*

▷ *What three strength-sapping lies did Samson devise?*
v7:
v11:
v13:

▷ *What did Delilah do each time? (v9, v12, v14)*

Surely, Samson isn't going to give in to Delilah. He knows full well that her design is to hand him over to the Philistines. But Samson was indulging his weakness for women. And he just couldn't stop.

👁 Read verses 15–22

▷ *How did Delilah break down Samson's defences? (v15–16)*

▷ *What took away Samson's strength? (v19–20)*

▷ *What did the Philistines do with him? (v21)*

▷ *But what began to happen? (v22)*

As a Nazirite, Samson was set apart to serve God, and showed his devotion by never cutting his hair. Once his hair was cut, the vow was broken, and he was no longer a Nazirite. And God would no longer give him great strength.

Samson was supposed to be set apart for God, putting God first in everything. But he put Delilah first, forgetting God. So God left him.

THINK ABOUT IT

▷ *Do you put God first in the way you live your life?*

▷ *What do you need to change so that your life is given to God?*

PRAY ABOUT IT

Talk to God about your weaknesses and the things that get between Him and you.

→ TAKE IT FURTHER

Find more on page 118.

60 Temple of doom

The Philistines have captured weak, baldy Samson and gouged his eyes out. It's time for them to celebrate and thank their god, Dagon, with Samson providing the entertainment.

👁 Read Judges 16 v 23–31

ENGAGE YOUR BRAIN

▶ *Who did they think was behind Samson's downfall? (v23–24)*

▶ *What was Samson's last request? (v26)*

▶ *And his final prayer? (v28)*

▶ *What did this final push achieve? (v30)*

Samson had messed up big time. He'd put women before God and had let his enemies overpower him. Instead of God getting the glory for Samson's strength, this fake god Dagon was being praised.

But Samson hadn't forgotten the Lord and called out to Him one last time. Even when we've let God down, we can still turn to Him. He still listens to us. Even though we disobey Him, God gives us far more than we deserve.

God answered Samson's prayers. Even if Samson's motives were not pure (v18), God's plans were still fulfilled — to punish His enemies and restore glory to His name.

Samson's death, brought a sort-of rescue for Israel. Christians now look back to Jesus' death which achieved a far greater rescue from the enemy, Satan, and his power.

PRAY ABOUT IT

Say sorry to God for specific times you've let Him down or brought disgrace to His name. Thank Him for forgiveness through Jesus and ask Him to use you in His plans despite your weakness.

→ TAKE IT FURTHER

Samson's strong points — page 119.

61 Spiralling out of control

Remember the circle pattern in Judges?

God's people turn to other gods

God lets their enemies defeat them

Israelites cry out to God

God sends a judge to rescue them

👁 Read Judges 17 v 1–6

ENGAGE YOUR BRAIN
▶ *Spot the mistakes...*
v1–2:
v3:
v4:
v5:
v6:

These were God's chosen people, but they were all living for themselves, not for God (v6). And when that happens, things can only get worse, as seen in this little story. Micah and his mother were not trusting in God; they were trusting God *and* manmade idols.

👁 Read verses 7–13
▶ *What offer did Micah make to this young Levite? (v10)*

▶ *What wrong assumption did Micah make? (v13)*

This whole story is a mess. Micah stole. His mum dedicated money to God but used it to make an idol to worship. And Micah made other stuff to worship and bring him luck. And he thought paying a priest to live with him would put him right with God. This all happened because the Israelites had no godly leader, so everyone did what they wanted (v6).

PRAY ABOUT IT
Without proper guidance, it's easy to stray away from God and think we know best. We don't. Say sorry to God for anything that's an idol in your life. Ask Him to help you listen to Christian leaders and live His way, not your own.

→ TAKE IT FURTHER
True religion on page 119.

62 ┊ Idol behaviour

A man called Micah was trying to do religion his own way — making his own idols and employing a Levite to be his live-in priest.

👁 Read Judges 18 v 1–13

ENGAGE YOUR BRAIN

▷ What are we constantly reminded in this part of Judges? (v1; 17 v 6)
▷ What did these warriors do right? (v5–6)

The Israelites had no king. God should have been their King but they were living for themselves, not for Him. They wanted His blessing (v5) and stayed religious, but it was false religion, worshipping idols and not obeying God. The tribe of Dan had gone against God's orders and failed to conquer Canaan (Judges 1 v 34), so went elsewhere to find somewhere easy to conquer.

👁 Read verses 14–21

▷ What did they do at Micah's place? (v17)
▷ What did the priest choose to do? (v19–20)

👁 Read verses 22–31

▷ What was Micah relying on? (v24)

▷ How would you describe the Danites? (v25–27)
▷ Who did the Danites worship? (v31)

The Danites must have felt smug — they now had their own territory, their own idols and their own priests. They probably thought God was on their side, yet theirs was false religion, not living God's way at all.

The hardest people to get through to with the gospel are the religiously satisfied. People who think they've done their bit, that God is pleased with them, yet they're not really serving God at all.

PRAY ABOUT IT

Pray for people you know who've created their own religious ideas but haven't turned to Jesus. Ask God to open their eyes and also to give you opportunities to share the gospel.

➜ TAKE IT FURTHER

More stuff on page 119.

63 | A moral mess

**The last few chapters of Judges show just how
far God's people had spiralled away from Him
— doing things their own way, not His.**

👁 Read Judges 19 v 1–21

ENGAGE YOUR BRAIN

- ▶ What are we reminded of in v1?
- ▶ How does the Levite's dad-in-law show great hospitality? (v3–9)
- ▶ Why didn't they stay in Jebus?
- ▶ Was Gibeah more friendly? (v15)
- ▶ Who gave them a place to stay?

👁 Read verses 22–30

- ▶ What shocking thing happened? (v22–25)
- ▶ What disgusting response did he make to the girl's murder? (v29)
- ▶ How did people react? (v30)

It seems unbelievable that such a horrific series of events could occur in Israel, among God's chosen people. They should have been living with Him as their King, but they ignored God and indulged in all kinds of sin. That's what happens when people refuse to live with God in charge.

It's easy to be blinded by the horrific nature of this story and miss the point it's making. These were God's people, and they were sinning against Him, because they were living for themselves, not Him.

GET ON WITH IT

- ▶ In what ways do you refuse to let God be the boss?
- ▶ What sin do you need to kick out?
- ▶ How will you make sure God is your King every day, in every area of your life?

PRAY ABOUT IT

Talk to God about what's really nagging at you today.

THE BOTTOM LINE

When God's not your boss, everything falls apart.

→ TAKE IT FURTHER

More moral musings on page 119.

Brother against brother

Yesterday we read the disgusting story of... actually, I'll let the Levite himself remind you of what happened.

👁 Read Judges 20 v 1–17

ENGAGE YOUR BRAIN

- ▷ *Who was there to hear the story? (v1–2)*
- ▷ *How did the Israelites respond to the Levite's story? (v10–11)*
- ▷ *What did they demand of the Israelite tribe, Benjamin? (v13)*
- ▷ *How did the Benjamites reply? (v13–14)*
- ▷ *How did the two armies compare? (v15–17)*

The unity of Israel here is impressive — gathering as one army to punish the people of Gibeah in Benjamin. But it's tragic that they were uniting to fight against another Israelite tribe. God's people were at such a low point, they were fighting each other.

The Benjamites stuck up for the people of Gibeah. They were vastly outnumbered but they would be no pushovers, with their 700 left-handed stone-slingers, who would cause havoc among the enemy who wouldn't be used to an attack from that angle.

👁 Read verses 18–25

- ▷ *What did the Israelites do right? (v18, v23)*
- ▷ *What were the suprising results? (v21, v25)*

It seems that God was punishing both Benjamin and the rest of Israel for rejecting Him. Even though the Israelites had turned to Him for guidance, the Benjamites came out on top in the first two battles. This reminds us that God's timing isn't the same as ours. When we turn to Him in prayer, things may not instantly go our way. But we can be sure His plans will work out in the end. The battle rages on tomorrow...

PRAY ABOUT IT

Talk to God about any Christians you're in conflict with.

➔ TAKE IT FURTHER

Battle against sin — page 119.

65 Leave me alone

The people of Gibeah (who were Benjamites) raped and murdered a girl, so the whole of Israel went to get revenge. Despite being hugely outnumbered, the Benjamites won the first two battles. Round three...

👁 Read Judges 20 v 26–48

ENGAGE YOUR BRAIN
▶ What did the Israelites do differently this time? (v26)

▶ What was there with them? (v27)

▶ What did God promise? (v28)

▶ What was the result?

▶ Who was behind it all? (v35)

This time, the Israelites showed they were serious about obeying God and needing His help — they fasted and offered sacrifices to God. Maybe after the first two defeats, Israel was repentant for its disobedience, pride and false religion. We're not told why their response was different and why God gave them victory this time, so we can only guess.

The Israelites had the ark of the covenant with them. The ark was the symbol of God's presence with His people. Despite all the setbacks and all their rebellion, God was still with them. But God wasn't with the Benjamites. That was the biggest punishment of all — God leaving them on their own.

Many people choose to be their own boss and ignore God. So the Lord gives them what they want and leaves them to ruin their own lives. There is no greater punishment than God leaving you. That's what hell is — eternal separation from God.

PRAY ABOUT IT
Pray for friends and family who choose to go their own way, not God's. Ask Him to show them the hopelessness of life without Him.

THE BOTTOM LINE
People who reject God get what they ask for — eternity without Him.

→ TAKE IT FURTHER
There's hope on page 120.

66 | Edge of extinction

The Israelites attacked the Benjamites and wiped out most of them. But their fury against Benjamin soon turned to sorrow for losing one of the twelve tribes of Israel.

Read Judges 21 v 1–14

ENGAGE YOUR BRAIN

▶ *What had the Israelite men promised in an oath? (v1)*

▶ *Why was this a problem? (v7)*

▶ *How did they solve the problem? (v11–12)*

▶ *But... what? (v14)*

The Israelites tried to wipe out Benjamin for its sin, but now they regretted it and were worried the Benjamites would die out completely. But they couldn't supply the Benjamites with wives because of the oath they'd made. The people of Jabesh-Gilead had refused to fight on the side of the Israelites, so they were punished — killing the men and capturing the female virgins for the Benjamites. Hideous, but they still didn't have enough wives.

Read verses 15–25

▶ *What was their next solution? (v20–21)*

▶ *What are we reminded at the end of Judges? (v25)*

In the last few chapters of Judges, we've seen God's people doing whatever they wanted (v25), rather than living God's way. They deserved to be wiped out by Him, but He was still with them. Unbelievable patience and love from God. Verse 25 reminds us they had no king. In the next issue of Engage, the story moves to 1 Samuel, and Israel gets a king...

PRAY ABOUT IT

How have you treated God badly recently, "doing as you see fit"? Admit these things to God. Thank Him for His incredible patience with you and ask for His help in living with Him as King of your life.

→ TAKE IT FURTHER

Judges review: page 120.

67 | PSALMS: Praise and panic

After the last few depressing days in Judges, we need to cheer ourselves up. So let's sing along with David in Psalms, discovering more about our incredible God.

👁 **Read Psalm 68 v 1–10**

ENGAGE YOUR BRAIN

▶ What does David pray for God's enemies? (v1–2)

▶ Why should God's people sing His praises? (v4–10)

👁 **Read verses 11–20**

▶ What else does God do for His people? (v19–20)

David is remembering God leading the Israelites to great victories over the kings of Canaan (v11–14), and is bursting with joy at God being present with His people (v15–18).

👁 **Read verses 21–27**

▶ What will happen to those who defy God? (v21)

▶ Who's at the front of this praise procession? (v27)

Recently we were reading how the tribe of Benjamin sinned horrifically

and were almost wiped out. Now we see them at the head of God's people. Despite their sin, the first king of Israel came from this tribe. God is ridiculously good to His people.

👁 **Read verses 28–35**

▶ Who should we be calling to sing God's praises? (v32)

▶ Why? (v33–35)

The beast (v30) might be Egypt and the bulls (v31) the surrounding countries. David looked forward to a time when all nations would recognise God as King. One day, they will!

SHARE IT

▶ How will you share your enthusiasm for God with your friends?

Ask the Lord to help you do it.

➔ **TAKE IT FURTHER**
More positivity on page 120.

79

68 | Pray when you're sinking

One of the best things about the psalms is the chance they give us to sit on someone's shoulder and listen as they pray. Do that now with David. He's having a tough time and it's getting him down. Deep down.

👁 Read Psalm 69 v 1–12

ENGAGE YOUR BRAIN

▶ How did David feel? (v1–3)

▶ What was getting him down? (v4)

▶ How were people treating him? (v7–12)

👁 Read verses 13–21

▶ What was David still sure of? (v13, v16)

▶ What did this make him do? (v14–18)

David prayed remembering what God is like. He knew God to be generous and trustworthy. And that shaped the way he prayed.

👁 Read verses 22–28

▶ What did David pray for? (v22–28)

▶ Why? (v26)

Can you imagine praying like this? Not without a huge dose of self-seeking revenge. But David clearly recognised God is fair — ultimately, He'll punish all who go against Him.

👁 Read verses 29–36

▶ How could David switch so quickly from sorrow (v29) to praise (v30)?

▶ Why should everyone praise God? (v33–36)

David was confident of God's faithfulness to His people. In this psalm, he began praying in desperation. But he ended by praising God and calmly trusting Him for the future.

PRAY ABOUT IT

Think what this psalm teaches us. And then take those truths into your prayer time.

→ TAKE IT FURTHER

Don't sink — swim to page 121.

69 | Quick! Help!

C'mon. Quick. Let's start. Now. Hurry. Move it.
Read on. This Psalm. Of David. Stands out.
For its urgency. Forget the formalities.
David goes straight to the point.

👁 **Read Psalm 70 v 1–3**

ENGAGE YOUR BRAIN

▶ *How did David react to his crisis? (v1)*

▶ *Why was David so desperate? (v2)*

▶ *What did he want from God? (v2–3)*

👁 **Read verses 4–5**

▶ *Despite his desperate situation, what did David want? (v4)*

▶ *What made David confident that God would rescue him?*

How do you respond to a crisis? Is it like this?
1. Panic
2. Say: "Why me?"
3. Try to solve it
4. Fail
5. Maybe think about praying

And even at this stage our prayers are often either...
1. "God, help! (though I'm not sure you actually will)". Or...
2. "God, do what I want. Right now, please".

▶ *How did David differ on both these counts as he prayed?*

Sure, he wanted help (against death threats, v2). But he knew God was reliable and trustworthy (v5). And, most of all, he wanted God to be honoured (v4).

TALK ABOUT IT

▶ *What should God's people always be excited about? (v4)*

▶ *What changes will this psalm make to the way you pray?*

➔ **TAKE IT FURTHER**
Help! Turn to page 121.

70 | Senior moment

Old age has a habit of showing people as they really are. Some people grow old in such a way we think: "I want to be like that when I'm old." Others make us hope we're not so self-centred.

👁 Read Psalm 71 v 1–8

ENGAGE YOUR BRAIN

The psalm writer (probably King David) is facing old age, looking back on a lifetime of knowing God's care.

- ▷ *Which verses here show his trust in God?*
- ▷ *And which show his thanks to God?*
- ▷ *What was it that gave him such confidence in the Lord? (v5)*
- ▷ *What can you look back on to remind you of God's care?*

👁 Read verses 9–18

- ▷ *What opposition was he facing? (v10–11)*
- ▷ *So what did he pray for? (v9, v12–13)*
- ▷ *And what did he resolve to do? (v14–18)*

What's old age for? Well, it's like the rest of life — we should use it to tell people how great God is. Whether young or old or in between, life is for singing God's praises and spreading the word about His Son Jesus.

👁 Read verses 19–24

- ▷ *What's impressive about this guy's attitude to God? (v20)*
- ▷ *What would he spend his old age doing? (v22–24)*

Wouldn't it be great to grow old like this man? He'd had a difficult life with many tough times, but he wasn't bitter, twisted or cynical. He still trusted God completely, knowing he was truly safe and secure with his God, who would restore his life.

GET ON WITH IT

- ▷ *How can you be like this old man while you're still young?*
- ▷ *Who will you tell about God's greatness?*

PRAY ABOUT IT

Use this psalm to fuel your prayers.

→ TAKE IT FURTHER

Try song writing on page 121.

71 Double vision

This psalm is about King Solomon — David's son, who ruled Israel wisely. But it's also about someone else. He's not mentioned by name but His character seeps out of almost every verse.

👁 Read Psalm 72 v 1–7

ENGAGE YOUR BRAIN

▷ *What did Solomon pray for? (v1)*

▷ *What would his reign be like, with God on his side? (v2–3)*

▷ *Who'd be protected and who'd be punished? (v4)*

👁 Read verses 8–14

▷ *How much greater would this king be? (v8–11)*

▷ *Strangely, what would make him great? (v12–14)*

👁 Read verses 15–20

▷ *What would such a king deserve? (v15)*

Solomon was the last great, godly king of all Israel. After him, it was mostly downhill for God's people as they rejected Him again and again. Solomon was a great and wise king but he wasn't perfect and gave into temptation and sin. But this psalm isn't only about him. It also points us to God's perfect King — Jesus.

▷ *How does Psalm 72 remind us of Jesus?*
v2:
v4:
v5:
v8:
v11:
v14:

PRAY ABOUT IT

Use those verses and v18–19 to praise God for sending His perfect, rescuing King.

→ TAKE IT FURTHER

Check out Isaiah on page 121.

Fighting slavery

William Wilberforce was born in 1759 in Hull in North-East England. His family were merchants trading with Russia and the Baltic States. He had a privileged background, going to Cambridge University before becoming the Member of Parliament for Hull at just 21. At this stage, William's biggest aim was to achieve personal success. He was close friends with the Prime Minister, William Pitt, and the two of them were big political celebrities. He didn't have a care in the world, and certainly saw no need for God in his life.

NEW DIRECTION

In 1784, Wilberforce's life changed radically. On a trip to Europe he spent time with one of his former school teachers, who was a Christian. They discussed faith and William read Christian books which challenged his beliefs. Soon he began to read the Bible and pray every morning and eventually gave His life to Jesus, committing his future work to serving God. William met the hymn writer John Newton who told Wilberforce: *"God has raised you up for the good of the church and the good of the nation, maintain your friendship with Pitt, continue in Parliament, who knows that but for such a time as this God has brought you into public life and has a purpose for you."*

The Abolition Committee — which was behind the campaign to abolish the slave trade — persuaded Wilberforce to champion their cause. Although it might seem incredible today, the slavers argued that theirs was a moral trade because they were trying to help people who'd been captured in African wars — who were otherwise going to be executed — and they were taking them to a safe place and a new life. Wilberforce's speech changed history. After delivering the shocking facts about slavery for a full three hours, he said to the lawmakers: *"Having heard all of this you may choose to look the other way but you can never again say that you did not know."*

TOUGH TIMES

Three years after Wilberforce's first speech, Parliament resolved to gradually abolish the slave trade. But a huge amount of Britain's wealth depended on it (in 1807, £17 million changed hands in the slave trade in Liverpool alone). Wilberforce was attacked in newspaper articles, physically assaulted, faced death threats and had to travel with an armed bodyguard. There were powerful vested interests determined to prevent any restrictions on slavery. "Gradual" abolition started to look like never.

Wilberforce had a nervous breakdown and his physical health collapsed. John Newton visited him and read the story of Daniel in the lions' den. Daniel, he explained, was a public man like Wilberforce, who found himself in great difficulty. But Daniel trusted in the Lord and though he had powerful enemies, none could defeat him because God was on his side. Newton told Wilberforce: *"The God whom you serve continually is able to preserve and deliver you, He will see you through."* This proved to be just the advice William needed.

SUCCESS AT LAST

Wilberforce's Abolition Bill became an annual occurrence as year after year he brought the issue before parliament. On the 23rd February 1807, abolition of the slave trade was once again debated in Parliament. When Wilberforce realised that the majority of the speeches were now in favour and that the Abolitionists were going to win, he bowed his head and wept. At 4 o'clock in the morning, the Commons voted by 283 to 16 to abolish the slave trade. It had taken twenty years to get this far. The capturing, transporting and selling of enslaved Africans was now illegal.

Although Wilberforce is most famous for his battle against the slave trade, he worked with the poor, he worked to establish educational reform, prison reform, health care reform and to limit the number of hours children were required to work in factories. Most of all he wanted to spread the gospel. He didn't just want people to go to church, He wanted to see people truly changed by Jesus, embracing a Christianity that would change the whole fabric of society.

72 : Acts: To be continued...

Earlier in Acts, we saw that the gospel has no ethnic boundaries and now we see it spreading to every section of society. But God has enemies who are keen to stop people hearing about Jesus.

👁 Read Acts 13 v 1–12

ENGAGE YOUR BRAIN

▷ *What do the prophets and teachers in Antioch have in common? (v1)*

Trick question! In some ways nothing but in another, everything! Look at the names for a minute. Barnabas we know about. Simeon, from his nickname, was probably a black African, as most likely was Lucius from Cyrene in North Africa. Manaen was an aristocrat from Herod's court, and then we have Saul, the former Pharisee and persecutor of the church. Very different people, but all chosen by God, all saved by the death of His Son and all brothers in Christ.

PRAY ABOUT IT

God shows His power when diverse people become family. Thank Him for the Christian brothers and sisters He's given you, and pray for His help to love them.

▷ *Who wants to speak to Saul and Barnabas? (v7)*

▷ *Who tries to stop them? (v8–10)*

▷ *Does Bar-Jesus/Elymas succeed?*

▷ *What happens to him?*

▷ *What happens to the proconsul?*

Behind every person who opposes the spread of the gospel is the devil. Does that shock you? The last thing the devil wants is people to turn to Jesus and have their sins forgiven. But God's enemies will never succeed. They can be obstructive and they can do real damage but they're ultimately doomed.

THE BOTTOM LINE

God's gospel will go out no matter what.

→ TAKE IT FURTHER

Continue to page 122.

73 | Plan A

People sometimes think what happened in Acts was something new, God's Plan B. But as we see in these verses, God's plan to bring salvation to the world has been His Plan A, right from the beginning.

👁 Read Acts 13 v 13–31

ENGAGE YOUR BRAIN

🄳 Where do Saul/Paul and his companions start as usual? (v14)

🄳 What key events in Israel's history does Paul refer to? List them below:

-
-
-
-
-
-
-
-
-
-

🄳 Who did God start His plan with? (v17, 26)

🄳 Did anything catch God by surprise? (v27)

🄳 How did God show that sin and death really were defeated? (v30)

🄳 What evidence do we have? (v31)

GET ON WITH IT

Faith isn't some vague thing — it's believing the message of trustworthy witnesses. Christianity isn't just another religion that might be "true for you" but not for everyone. It's God's plan from the beginning; predicted by the prophets and demonstrated through the life and death of Jesus Christ. Can you explain something of this to a friend?

THE BOTTOM LINE

God has a plan.

→ TAKE IT FURTHER

Here's the plan — go to page 122.

74 | A promise and a choice

Not only has God had His Plan A from the beginning, He's pointed to it all through Israel's history. Jesus' arrival should have been a major "Eureka!" moment for the Jewish people.

👁 Read Acts 13 v 32–41

ENGAGE YOUR BRAIN

▶ How did God fulfil His promises to the Israelites? (v32–33)

▶ How did God fulfil His promises to David? (v34–37)

▶ What wonderful blessing does Jesus' death and resurrection accomplish? (v38–39)

▶ Who is forgiveness offered to? (v39)

▶ What is the warning the Old Testament also offers? (v40–41)

The choice is clear and very very serious. Choose to believe Jesus or not. Forgiveness is offered to everyone who trusts in Jesus' death in their place. They are *justified* — it's just as if they'd never sinned. Only faith in Jesus brings forgiveness. Relying on yourself or keeping rules won't do it. Failure to trust in Jesus

means you'll perish (v41) — you face eternal death.

PRAY ABOUT IT

Thank God that Jesus is the King who lives forever. Thank Him that everyone who believes in Jesus can be forgiven and justified before God. Spend some time thanking God for bringing that saving message to you.

THE BOTTOM LINE

Jesus lives forever!

→ TAKE IT FURTHER

Face the challenge on page 122.

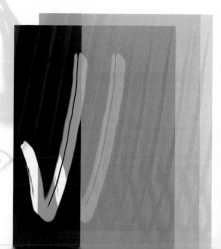

75 ┆ Share and beware

Paul and Barnabas took the message of Jesus to the Jews first. Their history and heritage were shouting out that Jesus is the promised King. Surely they would respond with gratitude and joy. Sadly, not many did...

◉ Read Acts 13 v 42–52

ENGAGE YOUR BRAIN

▶ *What are the positive signs at first? (v42–44)*

▶ *What do some of the Jews do, and why? (v45)*

▶ *What do Paul and Barnabas do next?*

▶ *Is this their plan or God's? (v46–47)*

▶ *How do the Gentiles respond? (v48)*

You might have thought from everything Paul and Barnabas had said so far that the good news was just for the Jewish people, but here we see God's grace to the whole world — part of His plan all along (v47).

▶ *What impact does the news about Jesus have? (v49)*
▶ *What else? (v50)*

TALK IT OVER

Have you noticed how evangelism often goes hand in hand with persecution? A friend becomes a Christian and her family dismiss her as a religious fanatic. You invite a friend to church and they laugh at you. Chat to another Christian about how you can get your expectations in line with what the Bible teaches in v48–50, and pray together to have the courage to share this life-changing message despite any opposition.

PRAY ABOUT IT

Read v52 again. Ask God to do the same for you as you live for Jesus and seek to share Him with others.

THE BOTTOM LINE

Expect opposition, but also expect the gospel to save people.

→ TAKE IT FURTHER

More useful stuff on page 122.

76 Gospel united

Amazing unity between Gentiles and Jews — it can only be the gospel. But it's not just believers who are brought together by the message of Jesus.

Read Acts 14 v 1–7

ENGAGE YOUR BRAIN

▷ *Where in Iconium did Paul and Barnabas start (as usual)?*

▷ *What were the results — good and bad? (v1–2)*

▷ *How does Luke (the author of Acts) describe the gospel message here? (v3)*

We've had loads of descriptions of the gospel message in Acts so far; *the good news about the Lord Jesus, the word of the Lord*, and now *the message of His grace*.

▷ *Why is this last one such a good way to describe the gospel?*

SHARE IT

Can you explain the good news about Jesus without using any jargon, any Christian-y language? Practise it now and pray for a chance to do it soon.

▷ *Does v5 remind you of anything?*

The last time we saw Jews and Gentiles collaborating in a plot like this it led to Jesus' execution. The gospel brings unity; for those who are being saved, a wonderful brotherhood — but for those who reject Christ, it creates new alliances with other enemies of the gospel.

▷ *Did all this opposition stop the gospel spreading? (v6–7)*

PRAY ABOUT IT

Ask for God's power and courage to keep talking about Jesus when things get tough.

THE BOTTOM LINE

The gospel brings unity of all kinds.

→ TAKE IT FURTHER

United we stand — page 122.

77 | Heard it all before

Ever get a feeling of déjà-vu, as if something's happened before? There's some of that today. Ever get a feeling...?

👁 Read Acts 14 v 8–20

Read through the three incidents in these verses and fill in the table below:

Verses	What happens?	Reminds us of...	Similarities/differences?
8–10		Acts 3 v 1–10 Luke 7 v 11–15 Mark 2 v 1–12	
11–18		Acts 12 v 21–23	
19–20		Acts 14 v 5 etc	

▶ In v11–18, how are Paul and Barnabas different to Herod?

▶ Why do you think this is?

Did you notice the way Paul and Barnabas speak to the pagan Lystranites? They still share the good news about Jesus but they start in a very different place from their synagogue routine with all its Old Testament references. Look at v15–17.

▶ Do you speak about Jesus in a way your friends will understand?

PRAY ABOUT IT

Ask God to help you talk bravely and understandably about Jesus.

THE BOTTOM LINE

Different places, different people. Same God, same plan.

→ TAKE IT FURTHER

More evangelism tips on page 123.

78 | Return journey

After all the travelling and excitement of people becoming Christians, it's time for some encouragement and a bit of reporting back to base — phew!

Read Acts 14 v 21–28

ENGAGE YOUR BRAIN

▷ What was the outcome of the Derbe visit (v21)?

▷ How did they make sure the disciples in Lystra, Iconium and Antioch were OK before they left? List what they said and did below (v22–23):

-
-
-
-
-
-

▷ Look at each of the points you've just listed. Why is each one so important?

PRAY ABOUT IT

We often attach a great deal of importance to our church or youth group leaders or older Christians, and to some extent that is right, as God has made them leaders of His people. But ultimately, it's God who will take care of us. See v23 and thank God that whatever happens, He will care for you if you've put your trust in Him.

▷ On returning to Antioch, what are we reminded about:
   a) how the work started? (v26)
   b) how the work was accomplished? (v27)

THE BOTTOM LINE

God saves us, keeps us and works through us by His grace.

→ TAKE IT FURTHER

Check your map on page 123.

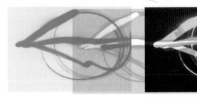

79 | The great debate

"Unless you do X, you can't be saved". Sadly, throughout history, people have tried to add something extra to the saving message of the gospel. What happened when this reared its head in the early church?

👁 Read Acts 15 v 1–11

ENGAGE YOUR BRAIN

▷ *What do the Jewish believers suggest is necessary to be saved? (v1, v5)*

▷ *Do Paul and Barnabas agree? (v2)*

▷ *How serious could this dispute become? What might the consequences be?*

▷ *What solution does the church propose? (v2)*

▷ *What do all the believers agree about? (v3b)*

Before you write this off as a blatantly ridiculous historical argument, think about the following: Have you ever heard or thought: "You can't be a Christian if you smoke / don't go to the right sort of church"?

▷ *What does Peter remind everyone about:*
   a) *God's choice? (v7)*
   b) *God's gift? (v8)*
   c) *God's work? (v9)*
   d) *God's salvation? (v11)*

▷ *How is anyone saved? (v11)*

PRAY ABOUT IT

Thank God for His grace and ask Him to forgive you for the times when you have thought that you or other people needed to do anything to contribute to their salvation. Only Jesus' death can rescue us — we can't earn it.

THE BOTTOM LINE

We are saved by God's grace through Jesus, and nothing else.

→ TAKE IT FURTHER

The debate continues on page 123.

80 | The great debate part II

So how will the "mother church" in Jerusalem handle this Jewish/Gentile debate? Peter has reminded them that everyone is saved by faith in Christ and not by obeying the Law of Moses. So what will the official line be?

👁 Read Acts 15 v 12–21

ENGAGE YOUR BRAIN

▶ What do Barnabas and Paul remind the assembly is happening? (v12)

▶ How does James explain that this has always been part of God's plan? (v13–18)

▶ What is his recommendation? (v19–21)

Notice James' concern is that they shouldn't make things difficult for the Gentile believers. He gives them a kind of diet version of the Law of Moses — to keep themselves unpolluted by other gods/idols, sex outside marriage or eating violently killed food.

👁 Read verses 22–35

▶ How does the church in Jerusalem decide to get this decision out? (v22–29)

▶ Who do they say is behind their letter? (v28)

▶ How do the Gentile believers respond? (v31)

▶ What else do Judas, Silas, Paul and Barnabas do? (v32–35)

This may seem like a little thing to us, but the inclusion of the Gentiles into the people of God was a massive thing back then and, even though we take it for granted, still is today.

PRAY ABOUT IT

Read 1 Peter 2 v 9–10 and then spend some time thanking God for His mercy to you, whether you're from a Gentile or Jewish background.

THE BOTTOM LINE

God does not want to make things difficult for His children.

→ TAKE IT FURTHER

A little bit more on page 123.

81 Barna' split

After all the positives of the last few chapters it's really sad to see Paul and Barnabas falling out here. They, like us, were human and imperfect. But God still used them (and uses us!).

👁 Read Acts 15 v 36–41

ENGAGE YOUR BRAIN

▶ What does Paul want to do? (v36)

▶ Is that a good plan?

▶ Where does the disagreement lie? (v37–38)

We're not told whether Paul or Barnabas is in the right here, but the outcome is surely not that great (v39).

▶ Nevertheless, what do Paul and Barnabas continue to do, despite going their separate ways?

▶ What will keep Paul and Silas (and us) going? (v40)

PRAY ABOUT IT

We are saved by God's grace, but we also live by God's grace. We need to depend on His undeserved kindness every day if we are to live for Him. Ask for that help now.

GET ON WITH IT

Are you annoyed with another Christian at the moment? You might be in the right or the wrong, but what really matters is your attitude.

Read Matthew 5 v 23–24 and Philippians 2 v 1–8.
Pray as you read them.
Then put them into practice!

THE BOTTOM LINE

God's grace keeps us going, despite our weakness.

→ TAKE IT FURTHER

Time to split — to page 123.

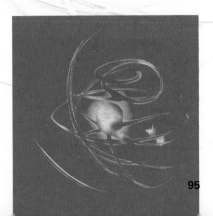

Isn't living a good life enough?

Being good gets you into the good books at school, at work, at home. So presumably doing good things is good enough to get you into heaven, right? That's what most people would suggest. What would you say? And more importantly, what does God say? Read on…

PERFECT WORLD

Imagine life in a perfect world: no difficulties, no disasters (personal or global), not even any death. Well, God's going to remake our world to be that kind of world (Revelation 21 v 4). *"Its brilliance [will be] like that of a very precious jewel"* (Revelation 21 v 11). Absolutely everything will be perfect; *"Nothing impure will ever enter"* (Revelation 21 v 27).

WORRYING NEWS

That's great news! But it's also worrying news. Because you and I are not perfect. We might do lots of good things, but we also do some not-so-good things, and even some totally not-good-at-all things. We're not perfect — so we can't be part of a world in which everything is perfect.

God puts it like this: *"All have sinned and fall short of the glory of God"* (Romans 3 v 23). All of us have failed to live God's way; none of us meet His perfect standard — we fall short.

FAIL!

Imagine taking an exam and the pass mark is 100%. As soon as you get one answer wrong, it doesn't matter how good you are at the rest, you can't pass. So with God's perfect standard — we've all done wrong, we've all missed the pass mark, and there's nothing we can do about it. However good we are, we're not good enough.

ENTER JESUS

You may be thinking this means no one deserves to be in God's perfect world — and you'd be right! That's why God's Son Jesus became human: to offer us what we don't deserve. Jesus' life was 100% perfect — He passed the exam — but instead of staying in heaven in perfection with God, He came to earth and died in agony on a cross. Why? *"God made him who had no sin to be sin for us, so that in him we might become the righteousness of God"* (2 Corinthians 5 v 21).

On the cross, Jesus took people's imperfection, their sins, upon Himself. He was shut out of God's presence instead of them. And He gave people His 100% perfection, His "righteousness", so they could have an undeserved place in God's perfect world. Wow!

GOOD OR SINNER?

Jesus once told a story about two guys, a religious leader and a tax collector (Luke 18 v 9–14). The leader prayed: *"God, I thank you that I am not like other men … I fast twice a week and give a tenth of all I get."* He was a really good guy — and he thought his goodness made him acceptable to God.

The tax collector was a traitor, a cheat, an outcast. Here's what he said: *"God, have mercy on me, a sinner."* He didn't think he was good enough. He knew he was a sinner.

Jesus said: *"This man, rather than the other, went home justified before God".* See, the "good" guy couldn't be good enough, and because he was relying on his own goodness, God didn't "justify" him (forgive him and give him eternal life). The second guy knew he wasn't good enough, so he relied on God, asking God to show mercy towards him. Anyone, however bad, can do that — everyone, however good, needs to do that.

So how do you see yourself. "Good", or "sinner"? It's only when we realise we can't be good enough that we can turn to Jesus and ask Him to give us His perfection so we can enjoy life with Him.

WHY BOTHER LIVING GOD'S WAY?

If we can't be good enough for God, why should we try to live His way? I could write a whole article in answer to this, but we don't have the space. So check out John 10 v 10, Ephesians 2 v 10 and 1 Thessalonians 4 v 1.

Zephaniah

God's day

Quickly write down everything you know about Zephaniah. If you're like me, it probably took you less than 5 seconds. Zephaniah's a mostly unknown prophet whose tiny book hides towards the end of the Old Testament. But he's a prophet who had a lot to say to God's people. And God will speak through him to us, all these centuries later.

Zephaniah was a prophet (spokesman for God) in Judah during the second half of the 7th century BC. Judah, with its capital Jerusalem, was all that was left of Israel. Judah was living dangerously. God's people were refusing to learn from God's judgment on the rest of Israel (which was destroyed in 722 BC). They behaved as if God didn't exist, as if they could ignore His word and get away with it, or as if He was just one of many gods.

It's to these people that God speaks, through Zephaniah. It wasn't a comforting message, but a warning. About a *"day of the Lord"* that was to come. God's day. A day when He would act in a very big way. We'll see from this book what God would do on God's day.

There would be irreversible, widespread destruction. But God would also act in line with His mercy. It's incredible stuff. Judgment and rescue. And we'll also see from the New Testament just what it means for us now to live in the light of God's day.

Zephaniah may be a small book, tucked away at the back of the Old Testament, with a name that's hard to pronounce. But underestimate it at your peril. Through it God speaks to us about His day. We'd better listen.

82 | Days of warning

Why should we listen to Zephaniah's words? Well, they're not simply his words — the very first sentence of the book tells us that this is "the word of the Lord". This is crucial stuff, so listen up.

👁 Read Zephaniah 1 v 1–3

▷ *What promise does God repeat? (v2–3)*

▷ *What exactly will He sweep away?*

▷ *What's the chilling line at the end of v3?*

God would act personally in devastating judgment against the world, and specifically against His people, Judah...

👁 Read verses 4–6

▷ *Who did God single out for punishment?*
v4:
v5a:
v5b:
v6:

These were God's chosen people, living in His city, yet they were chasing after false gods. It seems as if they'd worship anything — Baal, Molech, the stars — rather than following God alone. They were not even turning to God for help any more (v6). That's why He was going to wipe them out.

We may not openly worship idols, but we can secretly devote ourselves to more subtle gods — wealth, popularity, sport, fame, ambition. Like the people of Judah, we may even mix worshipping God with these things. As Zephaniah tells us, God doesn't take these things lightly.

PRAY ABOUT IT

Pray for people you know who worship other gods or the stars (astrology). Pray that they'd see the consequences of this and turn to the one true God. And talk to God about anything in your life that steals worship from Him.

THE BOTTOM LINE

God will punish anyone who turns away from following Him.

→ TAKE IT FURTHER

Prophet and loss on page 124.

83 | Day of terror

What's the scariest thing you've read? Which movies make you nervous? What fills your nightmares? Nothing is more terrifying than God's punishment. Maybe that's why we avoid thinking about it.

Read Zephaniah 1 v 7–13

ENGAGE YOUR BRAIN

▶ What would happen on God's day? (v8, v9, v12)

▶ What attitudes will the Lord punish? (v9, v12)

▶ What will be the result? (v10–13)

The Lord invited His people to a sacrifice but they would be the ones who were sacrificed (v7–8)! In the Bible we often read that where there's sin, there must be death. For believers, God provides a sacrifice — a substitute who dies in our place. But those who don't seek the Lord (v6) themselves become the sacrifice.

Read verses 14–18

▶ What will it be like when God pours out His anger? (v14–17)

▶ What can't save people from God's punishment? (v18)

Read Zephaniah 2 v 1–3

▶ What's the prophet's last-minute appeal? (v1)

▶ What three things must God's people seek? (v3)

Zephaniah's words came true — Jerusalem was turned to rubble. But this also points us to God's final day when He'll judge the world. There will be no escaping His punishment for those who've rejected Him. The only hope is to seek the Lord, to long for right living and to be humble before the God who can forgive us.

PRAY ABOUT IT

Read Zephaniah 2 v 3 again and pray through those things for people you know who desperately need Jesus.

→ TAKE IT FURTHER

What's all that about foreigners and thresholds? Turn to page 124.

84 ¦ Doom's day

Some geography tips to put today's reading on the map: Philisitia was south west of Israel, by the Meditteranean Sea; Moab and Ammon were east, across the Jordan; Cush is Egypt; Assyria was the other big superpower, also east.

👁 Read Zephaniah 2 v 4–7

ENGAGE YOUR BRAIN

▶ *How would you describe God's punishment of the Philistines? (v4–5)*

▶ *What hope was there for God's people in Judah? (v6–7)*

▶ *What was God's promise in the middle of judgment? (end of v7)*

👁 Read verses 8–11

▶ *What provoked God's anger? (v8, v10)*

▶ *How would God punish them? (v9, v11)*

▶ *What was the good news for God's people? (v9)*

👁 Read verses 12–15

▶ *What was Nineveh's (Assyria's capital) big mistake? (v15)*

▶ *What happened to it? (v13–15)*

It's terrifying stuff — God will ruthlessly punish those who are arrogant and insist on being the kings of their own lives, ignoring God. But in the middle of this horrific judgment there is hope (v7, v9). A faithful group (remnant) among God's people will be saved. Ultimately, this remnant came down to one person — Jesus Christ. Through His death and resurrection, He saved from punishment everyone who has faith in Him.

PRAY ABOUT IT

Talk to God about the sin you see all around you. Admit to Him your own sinful mistakes. Thank Him for offering hope in the middle of the darkness, through His Son Jesus.

THE BOTTOM LINE

Dark times are never hopeless for God's people.

→ TAKE IT FURTHER

More remnant stuff on page 124.

101

85 | Judgment day

Yesterday we saw God's punishment coming to all the nations around Jerusalem. But what about the people in Jerusalem itself? How had they been treating God and what would happen to them?

👁 Read Zephaniah 3 v 1–4

ENGAGE YOUR BRAIN

▷ What were the charges against Jerusalem?
-
-
-
-
-
-

👁 Read verses 5–8

▷ How is God totally different from His people? (v5)

▷ What should the people have learned from history? (v6)

▷ But how did they respond? (v7)

▷ What was the inevitable and chilling outcome? (v8)

God had destroyed the cities of His enemies. Jerusalem should have been the exception where His people obeyed Him, but it wasn't. So God will destroy the whole, sinful world.

It's tragic. God's people wouldn't imitate Him or obey Him, even though He does no wrong and offers them justice. God's people wouldn't trust God, even though He never fails.

When God gathers all the nations to judge them, all will be found guilty and punished. But that's not the last word from Zephaniah. Tomorrow he shows us that there *is* hope.

PRAY ABOUT IT

Confess your sin to God. Thank Him for His fairness in judgment. Pray for people who refuse to draw near to Him, as Jerusalem did.

THE BOTTOM LINE

God's judgment will be final.

→ TAKE IT FURTHER

There's no *Take it further* today.

86 ┆ Day of hope

What good could possibly come out of a day of judgment and punishment? Well, God's day would purify His people — removing all those who opposed Him and leaving a remnant who would live with Him as King.

👁 Read Zephaniah 3 v 9–13

ENGAGE YOUR BRAIN
▶ *What was God's great promise? (v9)*
▶ *Who was it for? (v10)*
▶ *Who would be removed from Jerusalem? (v11)*
▶ *How would this purify the city? (v11–12)*
▶ *What would it be like to be restored to God? (v13)*

An amazing turnaround for God's people. Now that's something worth shouting about...

👁 Read verses 14–20
▶ *What fears will be taken away? (v15)*
▶ *How is God's relationship with His people described? (v17)*
▶ *What great promises does God make? (v18–20)*

That's God's day. A day of judgment. And of rescue, too — God would keep a people for Himself, just as He'd promised. One day, God's people will enjoy all God's got for them. But how could God just take away their punishment?

On the cross, Jesus took God's judgment on Himself, for us. He died to rescue us from what we deserved. That means we can face God's final judgment day securely, knowing that Jesus has rescued us.

TALK ABOUT IT
▶ *What's the right attitude to have toward's God's judgment?*
▶ *What ongoing difference will Zephaniah make to you?*

PRAY ABOUT IT
Talk to God about what you've learned from Zephaniah about:
a) God
b) yourself
c) the world around you
d) God's day

→ TAKE IT FURTHER
More about the big day on page 124.

87 | Sense of perspective

"Surely God is good to Israel, to those who are pure in heart. But as for me, my feet had almost slipped ... for I envied the arrogant when I saw the prosperity of the wicked." (Psalm 73 v 1–3). Time for a perspective check.

👁 Read Psalm 73 v 4–14

ENGAGE YOUR BRAIN

▷ *What are the characteristics of the godless rich? (We counted 12 of them.)*
▷ *What do they think about God? (v11)*
▷ *Why does this get the writer (Asaph) down? (v12–14)*

👁 Read verses 15–20

▷ *What made him change his mind? (v17)*
▷ *What's the reality for people who reject God? (v18–20)*

👁 Read verses 21–28

▷ *What had caused this guy to lose his sense of perspective? (v21–22)*
▷ *But what great truths can believers cling on to? (v23–26)*
▷ *How does he compare those who are right with God and those who aren't? (v27–28)*

Ever wonder if all your non-Christian friends are right and you're wrong?

This psalm writer did. This guy was looking around the world instead of looking up to heaven. He lost his godly perspective. It's easy to do. We see others seemingly better off and more happy than we are. We start to resent it and doubt God's promises.

But everything isn't as it seems. God will punish those who reject Him, however successful they seem. They'll perish. We were all heading for that punishment. But for those of us who've accepted the forgiveness offered by Jesus, the future is far brighter. God holds our hand, guiding us. He's all we need and He's leading us into glory.

PRAY ABOUT IT

Lord, please keep me thinking clearly and with a godly attitude. Thank you for your generosity and mercy toward me. Please help me to tell others about your love for us.

➡ TAKE IT FURTHER

A fresh perspective on page 124.

88 | Temple of gloom

This psalm was written after the vicious Babylonian army trashed Jerusalem — including the temple, the place of God's presence with His people. This is a sorrowful prayer song to God.

👁 **Read Psalm 74 1 v–11**

▶ *Why was the writer massively upset? (v1–2)*

▶ *What had happened? (v3–8)*

▶ *What made the situation unbearable? (v9)*

▶ *And what was even worse? (v10–11)*

The writer recognised that God had punished His people. But how could God *still* punish His own people, even Zion (Jerusalem) where His temple was. Wasn't He breaking His word, ruining His plan? Not at all. His own people had abandoned Him, but it wasn't the end of the story. As always, there was still hope for the faithful few.

👁 **Read verses 12–23**

▶ *What did the writer remember about God? (v12–14)*

▶ *What else? (v15–17)*

▶ *So what did He ask God? (v19, v22)*

▶ *What would be the result? (v21)*

When God seemed silent, when the goodness of God was called into question, this man clung on to:
• God's character and power (v12–17)
• God's faithfulness to His promises (the covenant, v20)
• God's care for His people (v19)
• God's concern to defend His reputation (v22)

PRAY ABOUT IT

When life seems too tough, Christians can cling on to these same things. We can be certain that God listens to us, even when He seems distant. With those things at the front of your mind, talk to God now.

➡ **TAKE IT FURTHER**

Appetite for destruction — page 125.

89 | Don't stick your neck out

Point your cow horns down and stop stretching your neck out! Confused? Hopefully you won't be after we've sung along with Psalm 75.

👁 Read Psalm 75 v 1–3

ENGAGE YOUR BRAIN

▶ *What were God's people thankful for? (v1)*

▶ *What must we remember about God's judgment? (v2)*

▶ *What should we remember when the world's falling apart? (v3)*

When we look at the world around us, it's easy to panic. But, through the Bible, we know all about God's character ("Name") — He's totally fair and completely in charge. And He's near us through His Son and through His Holy Spirit.

👁 Read verses 4–10

▶ *What's the message to proud people? (v4–5)*

▶ *What's the message to people who reject God? (v6–8, v10)*

▶ *If we're on God's side, what should we do? (v9)*

A mooving picture. If a cow or ox lifted up it's horns or stretched out its neck, it was refusing to be harnessed by its master. This psalm is a warning to people who reject God ruling their lives. God is the Judge. He rules. Don't think you can take God on; eventually He'll show you who's boss.

God judges fairly and in His own time (v2). He will punish the proud and everyone who opposes Him. And His judgment is unstoppable (v8).

PRAY ABOUT IT

Pray for stiff-necked people you know. And use verse 1 to praise our perfect, fair, all-powerful God.

→ TAKE IT FURTHER

No *Take it further* today.

90 | The fear

God defended His people in His city
(Jerusalem/Salem/Zion) against enemy
attack. Here's their tuneful response.

👁 Read Psalm 76 v 1–9

ENGAGE YOUR BRAIN

▶ *What did God do for His people?*
(v3)

▶ *How exactly did God show His*
power? (v5–6, v8–9)

▶ *How should His enemies view*
Him? (v7)

We've heard loads about God's
judgment in this issue of *engage*.
In this Old Testament battle, God
punished those who opposed Him
and rescued those who cried out to
Him for help. The New Testament tells
us it will be the same on the final Day
of Judgment, when Jesus returns.

👁 Read verses 10–12

▶ *How should people respond to*
this powerful, terrifying God?
(v10–12)

Through His Old Testament people,
God made Himself known, in acts of

judgment and rescue. Through Jesus,
God has now made Himself known in
person. One day, everyone will submit
to God as their King. Some willingly
— His people, Christians. Others
unwillingly — those who reject Him.
This psalm shows us the right way to
respond to God.

▶ *How would you sum it up?*

▶ *What will you change today to*
show you've grasped this?

PRAY ABOUT IT

Think about what God's taught you
through the books we've looked at
in this issue of *engage*. What do you
need to talk to Him about? What
have you learned about Him? What
can you thank Him for?

➔ TAKE IT FURTHER

Write your own psalm on page 125.

If you want a little more at the end of each day's study, this is where you come. The TAKE IT FURTHER sections give you something extra. They look at some of the issues covered in the day's study, pose deeper questions, and point you to the big picture of the whole Bible.

1 THESSALONIANS
Ready for Jesus?

1 – CHRISTIANITY IN CONFLICT
Read 1 Thessalonians 1 v 2–3

▶ *How often did Paul pray for these Christians?*

▶ *How often do you pray for other Christians?*

▶ *Why is it important to pray for them?*

Make a list of your Christian friends. Use it to pray for them regularly and thank God for what He's doing in their lives. And talk about it together more often.

2 – WORD POWER
Read verses 6–7 again

▶ Who can you imitate?

▶ How?

▶ How can you be a role model to younger Christians?

▶ What would that involve you doing?

▶ What would you need to cut out of your life?

3 – FAIR SHARE
Maybe you care for younger Christians in a church club or youth group, or you've got younger brothers or sisters. Think of younger Christians you know, then re-read v8–12 replacing "we" with "I", "our" with "my" and "us" with "me". How true does it sound? Keep Paul's example as a checklist for yourself in the weeks ahead.

4 – WORD'S WORTH
Read verses 15–16
The people who put Jesus to death have earned God's anger and will be punished when Jesus returns as Judge. That's true of everyone who rejects Jesus. Everybody needs to be rescued by Him (v16): both Jews and Gentiles (non-Jews).

Does this bring anyone to mind? Friends or family members who need Jesus? Now's a good time to get praying for them.

5 – MISSING PEOPLE
Read 1 Thess 2 v 17 – 3 v 7 again

▶ *What different emotions do we see from Paul?*

▶ *What do they tell us about him?*

▶ *What do these verses tell us about guidance?*

▶ How did Paul make decisions?

▶ What did he do when things seemed to get in his way?

▶ What can you learn from Paul?

6 – THESSALONIAN THRILL

Read verses 6–10 again

Paul regularly reminded new Christians that it wasn't going to be easy; there would be opposition both from the devil and other trials (see v3 and v5 earlier).

▶ But is Paul depressed about this? (v7–10)

▶ In the middle of his own persecution, what encourages him?

7 – LET'S TALK ABOUT, UMM, THINGY

Read verses 3–4 again

These verses are worth memorising. And definitely worth obeying.

▶ What sexually immoral thoughts/ actions will you now avoid?

▶ What wrong habits do you need to break?

Read verses 9–10

There's always further progress for us to make, whatever stage of the Christian life we're at. As if Paul is saying: You may be doing well, but God wants you to do even better. Catch the emphasis here on unselfishness and growth, and ask God to help you change more and more.

8 – MORE LOVE, LESS NOISE!

Read verse 11 again

This literally means: *"Make it your ambition to have no ambition."*

Calm down and get on with some work humbly and quietly.

▶ How does this alter your thinking about jobs, careers etc?

▶ Does your everyday life win the respect of outsiders?

▶ How could the way you live be a better witness to outsiders?

9 – BACK TO THE FUTURE

Read verse 13 again

▶ What makes Christians different from others when it comes to facing up to the death of Christian friends/family?

For Christians, death is like sleep. It's temporary. Christians who have died will be "woken up" again to be with Christ forever. Will you make a point of remembering this?

▶ How should it affect the way you live?

10 – DAY RETURN

A guy called John Stott said: *"There are two reasons why people are taken by surprise when a burglar breaks in. The first is that he comes unexpectedly during the night, and the second is that the householder is asleep. We can do nothing about the first reason, but we can about the second."*

▶ How can you prepare yourself for Jesus' return?

Pray for any friends or family who are unprepared to meet Jesus when He returns.

11 – CHECK IT OUT
Read verse 14 again.
Then read Romans 15 v 1–7.

▶ *Why should we help out "weaker" Christians and not just please ourselves? (v3–4)*

▶ *What help will we get? (v5–6)*

▶ *How can you put v1–2 and v7 into action?*

12 – GOODBYE AND GOD BLESS
Read 1 Thess 5 v 12–24 once more
Are there too many commands here to take in? Well you can take heart from Paul's prayer (v23) and God's promise (v24).

▶ *How does this encourage you to get started on obeying what's there in v12–22?*

▶ *Is there one command that stands out now?*

If so, tackle that today and ask God to help you with the others, too. Make sure you keep coming back to these verses.

JUDGES
Heroes and zeroes

13 – SO FAR, SO GOOD
Read verses 11–15 again
Whenever you read something in the Bible that seems a bit strange, always ask the question: *"Why did God put it there?"*

This little story seems a bit out of place. But God isn't random. Perhaps it's a little pic of the whole story: Caleb keeps his promise to Othniel. God keeps His promises too (Israel were in the promised land, despite all their rebellion). But the problem is that, unlike Othniel, God's people don't respond to Him as they should. As Judges will show us in detail.

15 – ROUND AND ROUND
Judges 2 v 10–23 sets up the whole book. It's not just a story, it explains what's going on in terms of God's action and purpose.

Read Judges 2 v 18–19
The whole book will be a series of mini rescues!

Read Judges 3 v 1–6

▶ *Rather than learning to worship false gods, what should God's people have learned?*

▶ *Are there times when you're sad rather than sorry for the things you've done which offend God and others?*

▶ *Can you think of examples?*

If we're just sad because we've been found out, then we're in danger of going round and round in circles like the Israelites. As we'll see, their circles grew wider and wider, taking them further away from God.

16 – JUDGE NUMBER ONE
Read verses 7–9 again

▶ *What is the trigger which leads God to act?*

That's what God's waiting for. We need to see our need. We need to be distressed by the trouble our sin gets us into. We need to be deeply discontented with the oppression of the enemy. We need to cry out to the Lord to rescue us, knowing that He alone can.

17 – EGLON HIS FAT FACE
Read Judges 3 v 31

That's all we learn about Shamgar! Even Bible experts are baffled by him. They think Shamgar might not even have been an Israelite due to his weird name. They're not even certain if he was son of a guy called Anath, or a worshipper of the fake goddess Anath or from the town of Ben-Anath.

We do know that he used an unusual weapon to bash the Philistines. An ox-goad was a big, long stick with a pointy bit for prodding oxen in the right direction and a spade for cleaning the muck from the ploughs.

The most important thing we know is that: "*He too saved Israel*". Even though we know very little about Shamgar, God used him to save His people! God often uses surprising people and methods to do the incredible. That's how powerful God is. He can even use sinful weaklings like us! What a God!

18 – HERE COME THE GIRLS
**Read verse 8 again
and then Hebrews 11 v 32–34**

In the Judges chapter 4, Barak comes across as a coward who needs brave Deborah to hold his hand. But Hebrews 11 tells a different story. He's included in a list of heroes of faith!

How incredibly encouraging is that? You might have thought God would have dismissed Barak as an untrusting wimp after v8. But no, God — and Deborah — persevere with him. And then look what happens next time Barak is told to "go" (v 14). Faith and courage in large measure now! Only God can transform us like that.

19 – DEBORAH: THE MUSICAL
Read verse 8 again

Without the word of God, people went astray.

▶ *In what ways?*
▶ *And how do we?*
▶ *Can you give an example from your own experience?*
▶ *What do you need to talk to God about, right now?*

20 – INVADED

Ever cry out to the Lord in complaint and distress, asking Him to rescue you from trouble and tough times? But do you ever recognise the possibility that your own sin might be the cause? Maybe you need to repent of what has been wrong.

As you talk to God now, admit the ways you've turned away from Him recently. Be brutally honest, and ask for His help.

21 – MIGHTY WEAKLING
Read verse 16 again

Again and again in the Bible, God reassures His nervous, hesitant people with these words. Check out some of these examples:

Genesis 28 v 10–15
Exodus 3 v 1–12
Psalm 23 v 4
Matthew 28 v 16–20
Acts 18 v 1–11

22 – CHOOSING SIDES
Read Romans 8 v 31–39

Whoever might be against us, God is greater, and He won't abandon us or let us go. Because He loves us so much.

▶ *What do you find most encouraging in v35–39?*

Whatever the opposition, danger or difficulties that tempt us to give up, nothing will separate us from Jesus' love, or from sharing in His victory (v37).

▶ *What things are you most afraid of?* Add them to Paul's list in v38–39. And thank God that not even those things can stop His plans or His love for you.

23 – GIVE FLEECE A CHANCE

Ever heard Christians say they're *"hanging out a fleece"* to check God's guidance, as Gideon did? *"Lord, if my trousers turn green when I've finished praying, then I'll move to Guatemala."* It's not the best way to do things. God was kind enough to be patient with Gideon's doubt and nervous

requests, but he should have trusted God's great promises to him.

Keep looking out for God's promises in the Bible. Hang on to them. Act on them. In chapters 7 and 8, Gideon does act in faith, trusting in God's promises.

▶ *How do you need to rely less on yourself and more on God?*

24 – GOD'S 300
Read verse 16 again,
then 2 Corinthians 4 v 5–7

Christians are the jars of clay here — brittle, but they carry the powerful light of the gospel. We're sinful and often pathetic and useless. Yet God uses us to spread the news of His Son Jesus and the rescue He offers. We shouldn't take the credit — all the glory goes to God.

25 – CATCH SOME ZS
Read verses 1–3
and Proverbs 15 v 1

▶ *Who do you need to be more gentle and less argumentative with?*

Now read Philippians 2 v 1–11

▶ *How should people united to Christ treat each other? (v2)*
▶ *What is the key to unity? (v3–4)*
▶ *How far did Jesus go in His humble service of others? (v8)*
▶ *Where is Jesus now? (v9)*
▶ *How does that encourage a church suffering for Christ?*
▶ *How will you change your attitude and behaviour to other Christians in the light of Jesus' example?*

27 – TREES TEASE
Read 1 Timothy 3 v 1–7
In the New Testament, leaders are called overseers and elders and deacons. Different words, but all leaders.

- *Why is this kind of leadership called a "noble task"? (v1)*
- *What must leaders be like and what must they do? (v2–7)*
- *Why must they have a good reputation outside the church?*
- *What qualities would you look for in a Christian leader?*
- *What qualities do we tend to (wrongly) look for first?*
- *How do these verses alter your attitude to your leaders?*

28 – ABIMELECH ABOLISHED
Sometimes it seems as though evil people and evil forces can do as they wish in the world.
But read Colossians 2 v 15
Jesus defeated the power of evil by His death on the cross.
Read 2 Thessalonians 1 v 5–10

- *Is God's judgment and punishment fair? (v5–6)*
- *What will happen to those who persecute God's people? (v6)*
- *And to believers? (v7)*
- *When will all this happen? (v7, v10)*

PSALMS
29 – SOUL MATE
For the whole story of Absolom murderously chasing David, read 2 Samuel chapters 15–18.

30 – WORDS AND SWORDS
Check out what these proverbs say about words. Pick the one that best applies to you and learn it by heart.
Proverbs 10 v 19
Proverbs 12 v 25
Proverbs 15 v 1
Proverbs 16 v 24

32 – SHOUT!
Quite a few Bible experts think Psalm 66 is talking about God's brilliant rescue of His people from the Assyrians. Check it out.

Read 2 Kings chapter 18
- *What made Hez different from other kings? (v5)*
- *What was the result? (v7–8)*
- *What disaster struck? (v13)*
- *What did Hez do at first? (v14–16)*
- *Did it work?*
- *What did the enemy army chief claim? (v33–35)*

Read 2 Kings chapter 19
- *How did Hez react? (v1)*
- *How did God encourage Hezekiah? (v5–7)*
- *What's great about Hezekiah's prayer? (v14–19)*
- *What did God promise Hez? (v29–34)*
- *How were God's people rescued? (35-37)*

33 – SMALL BUT TASTY
**Read Matthew 5 v 14–16
and 1 Peter 2 v 9–10**

▷ *What are the implications of these
verses for your life?*

ACTS
To be continued...

34 – TRANSFORMER

Not had a "Damascus road" experience?
Does that mean you're not a proper
Christian? No, Saul's experience isn't the
norm. But becoming a follower of Jesus
always includes a personal encounter with
Him: repenting, submitting to Him as boss
of your life, trusting Him, and being asked
to serve Him.

▷ *How did you turn to Jesus?*
▷ *How are you serving Him now?*

Think of some of your really anti-God,
non-Christian friends.

▷ *Do you expect God to be able to
change even them?*
▷ *Do you pray for that?*

35 – GO, SAUL, GO!

Notice verse 31 of chapter 9. The same
Saul/Paul encourages us to pray for our
governments in 1 Timothy 2 v 1–4 for the
same reason:
*"I urge, then, first of all, that requests,
prayers, intercession and thanksgiving
be made for everyone — for kings and
all those in authority, that we may live
peaceful and quiet lives in all godliness*

*and holiness. This is good, and pleases
God our Saviour, who wants all men to
be saved and to come to a knowledge
of the truth."*

Pray for your government right now.

36 – SAINTS AND SINNERS
Read verses 36–39

▷ *What characterised the way Dorcas/
Tabitha lived as a follower of Jesus?*
▷ *How can you live out your love for
Jesus in a similar way where you are?*

Read verse 43

Did you miss the shock? Peter, a Jew, is
staying with a tanner (leather worker).
That's someone who was close to all kinds
of dead animals, which any Jew would
have regarded as "unclean". Contact with
them would have made you unfit for God.
So a big surprise that Peter stayed with
him. But this is just a taste of what Peter's
got to learn in the next chapter.

37 – BELLY VISION

If you are reading this, it's most likely
you're a Gentile, a non-Jew. You would
have had no place in God's family.

**But read Ephesians 2 v 11–13 and
19–21** and marvel at what God has done.
And if you do have Jewish ancestry —
read Ephesians 2 v 14–18 and praise
God for His grace shown to all.

38 – NO FAVOURITES

**Read Ephesians 6 v 9,
Colossians 3 v 25,
and Deuteronomy 10 v 17–19**

God doesn't judge people according to their looks, accent, background, nationality, education, upbringing etc.

▷ *Do you?*

▷ *On what basis does God save/judge people? (Acts 10 v 35)*

40 – SUSPICIOUS MINDS

You might like to get hold of a copy of *Operation World* to help you pray for other countries, or see www.operationworld.org for daily prayer points and updates.

41 – READY STEADY GROW

Read verses 27–30 again

▷ *How did these new Christians live out their faith? (v29–30)*

It wasn't two separate churches — a Jewish one and a Gentile one — but one church family in two different places. They belonged to each other and cared for each other. So these guys happily helped out the hard-up Jewish Christians.

Pray that you'd imitate their witness, encouragement and responsibility of caring for other Christians.

42 – PETER, PRAYER & PERSECUTION

Have you ever read anything about Christians who died for their faith? An oldie but a classic is *Foxe's Book of Martyrs*. Try getting hold of a copy

(or read bits of it online) and dip into it to be inspired by people who God helped to stand firm until the end.

43 – HEROD HUMBLED

Atheist philosopher Nietzsche once declared *"God is dead."* When this appeared as graffiti at a university; *"God is dead – Nietzsche"*, someone wrote underneath *"Nietzsche is dead – God"*. One of the biggest dangers we face as human beings is arrogance — check out Psalm 103 for a corrective.

LAMENTATIONS
Down but not out

44 – JERUSALEM JUDGED

Jeremiah probably wrote Lamentations, though we don't know that for certain. The book has a pattern to it. Each chapter (except chapter 5) is written as an acrostic — each verse begins with a letter of the Hebrew alphabet, in order. Chapter 3 has 3 verses for each letter. It's expressing the people's grief in full, from A to Z.

45 – CONSEQUENCES OF SIN

**Read Deuteronomy 28 v 15–19
and then v 49–63**

▷ *What warnings did the Israelites receive?*

▷ *What do you think it means to "revere this glorious and awesome name"?*

▷ *How should Israel have done this?*

▷ *How can you show God more respect?*

▷ *How can you make sure you avoid the*

mistakes the Israelites made?

46 – GOOD GRIEF

**Read verse 38 again
and then Romans 8 v 28
and finally John 3 v 16**

▶ *How do these verses encourage you
as you live in a world where evil and
suffering are so obvious?*

47 – AGGRESSIVE PRAYER

Lamentations chapter 3 touches on God's
faithfulness to His people. The New
Testament goes into much more depth on
the subject.

Read Romans 8 v 31–39

▶ *Answer each of the questions.*
v31:
v32:
v33:
v35:

▶ *How do v37–39 sum up the answers?*

▶ *How does Romans chapter 8 respond
to the suffering and misery of God's
people in Lamentations?*

48 – WRECKED BY SIN

Edom also shows up in the book of
Obadiah. It's only one chapter long, so...
Read Obadiah v 1–21

▶ *How did Edom treat the Israelites?
(v10–14)*

▶ *What is predicted for Edom by
Obadiah?*

▶ *How is this similar to Lamentations
4 v 21–22?*

▶ *How will Edom's punishment be
worse than Israel's?*

Edom was proud and arrogant, thinking
they were completely safe. The danger in
feeling secure and safe is that you think
things will never change, and that you're
responsible for your success. The message
Obadiah brought to God's people was
intended to comfort them: God would
judge the Edomites for their pride. But it
was also a reminder to them not to get
arrogant, too.

In Jesus' death, God showed His judgment
on sin. His final judgment, sorting out
all wrong, is still to come. So, Christians
must keep going till then trusting Jesus.
And not get proud — God's not interested
in those who think they can offer Him
something, but in those who know they
can't and so must rely on Him to rescue
them. Be dependent on Him.

49 – THE END?

**Read verses 20–22 again
and then 1 Peter 3 v 18**

Unlike the writer of Lamentations, we live
after Jesus died on the cross. Imagine you
could go back in time. How would you use
this verse to explain to the Lamentations'
writer how Jesus has restored the
relationship between God and those who
turn to Him?

JUDGES

50 – HEROES AND ZEROES

**Read verses 6–8 again
and then Mark 8 v 34–38**

▶ *What does Jesus say about trying to be on both sides?*

▶ *How do you do that sometimes?*

▶ *Who are you living for?*

Jesus asks no more of His followers than what He went through Himself. To give yourself completely to Him, just as He did for you by dying for you.

▶ *But is it worth it? Pick out the promises and warnings Jesus gives in v35–38.*

51 – JUDGE JEPHTHAH

The way the people treated Jephthah is a picture of the way they treated God. Compare chapters 10 and 11:

	ch10	ch11
Rejection	v6	v1–3
Trouble	v7–9	v4
Repentance	v10	v5–6
Refusal	v11–14	v7
Request	v15–16	v8
Acceptance	v16	v9–11

▶ *Similarly, do you only turn to God in a crisis?*

53 – GIVE GOD THE GLORY

**Read verses 1–4 again
and then Judges 8 v 1–3**

▶ *What's the difference between Jephthah and Gideon's responses?*

▶ *And how were the outcomes different?*

Now read Ephesians 4 v 1–6

▶ *What does Paul want us to do? (v1)*

▶ *What five qualities should Christians show? (v2)*

▶ *How hard should we try to get along with other Christians? (v3)*

▶ *Which of the five qualities do you need to work on most?*

▶ *Who do you need to be more united with?*

Talk these things over with God now.

54 – ANGEL DELIGHT

Samson's lifestyle was to be totally different from others to show he was set apart for God. And the Israelites were God's chosen people, and so they were expected to live differently from the godless nations around them.

Read Deuteronomy 4 v 5–8

▶ *If God's people obeyed His laws, what impact would it have?*

This is true for Christians too. Because of Jesus, God is close to us, His people. When you obey God's words (in the Bible), people around you will get a glimpse of your relationship with God. Your lifestyle will shape their view of God. That's why it's vital we read, understand and obey God's word.

56 – ROARS, RIDDLES AND RELATIVES

Don't follow Samson's example here! Don't chase after what you want, not thinking about whether it's the right thing and what God wants. But if you have gone the wrong way, then take heart! God is still in control, and He can use your most disastrous decisions to achieve His purposes. Though don't use that as an excuse just to do whatever you want.

Read Romans 8 v 28

God can use even our mistakes for His good purposes and for our good. Think about times when mistakes you've made have led to you learning big lessons from God or changing your ways.

57 – FOX TAILS AND DONKEY JAWS

Read verse 18 again
followed by Hebrews 11 v 32–34

The key to understanding Samson is that, for all his glaring faults, he was still a man of faith. Samson knew who to rely on for his strength, when no one else was prepared to stand with him.

▶ *Do you?*

I guess we don't normally need miraculous muscle power, but don't we often need strength and courage to do things we know are impossible without God?

58 – STRENGTH AND WEAKNESS

Read 1 Corinthians 6 v 15–20

▶ *Why is what we do with our bodies so important?*
▶ *Why is sex outside marriage a big deal? (v16)*
▶ *What should we aim for instead? (v17)*
▶ *What's the only safe option? (v18)*
▶ *Why? (v18)*
▶ *Why? (v19)*
▶ *Why? (v20)*
▶ *So... what do YOU need to do?*

59 – HAIR TODAY, GONE TOMORROW

Read verse 17 again

Samson knew it was not his hair itself that gave him strength — that was just the sign of his devotion to God as a lifelong Nazirite. He must have known he was committing spiritual adultery; cutting off his relationship with God and devoting himself instead to Delilah.

Read James 1 v 14–16 and 4 v 4

James is very blunt with us: *"You adulterous people, don't you know that friendship with the world is hatred towards God?"*

Whether it's your sexuality or whatever the world entices you with, will you commit spiritual adultery by letting it win first place, God's place? We must reject temptation right from the beginning. Few people fall without gently slipping first.

60 – TEMPLE OF DOOM
Read verse 28 again
The name *Sovereign Lord* is the name Israel associated with God's rescue of them from Egypt (Exodus 3 v 14–17).

▶ *Which events in history give us confidence to call on the name of God? To turn to Him for help?*

God used Samson to rescue His people from their enemy. It wasn't a complete rescue, but it does show God working His purposes and plans out.

▶ *Why is Jesus' rescue so much greater?*

61 – SPIRALLING OUT OF CONTROL
Micah's actions seem ridiculous but many people add their own bits to Christianity to satisfy themselves. But it's a big mistake to concentrate on being religious and forget what Christianity is all about — Jesus Christ.

Read James 1 v 22–27
▶ *What is not true Christianity? (v22–24)*
▶ *What is? (v25)*
▶ *What must Christians make sure they do? (v26)*
▶ *So what is true religion? (v27)*

We could choose to ignore dentists' orders and not brush our teeth. We're free to do so. But we know the end result would be decay and pain. See the point? Get away from thinking that living God's way will cramp your style, or make life dull.

Don't add your own ideas to Christianity, stick with what's in the Bible. Obey it. Try to live as Jesus did. That's true Christianity.

62 – IDOL BEHAVIOUR
Read Judges 1 v 34 and 18 v 1–2
The tribe of Dan wrongly thought they could find something better than the land God told them to conquer and live in.

▶ *In what ways do you try to take things into your own hands instead of doing things God's way?*

63 – A MORAL MESS
Read Genesis 19 v 4–11
▶ *How do the Israelites compare with the people of Sodom and Gomorrah?*
▶ *Why is this so shocking?*

These horrifying chapters are written deliberately to offend us. We should react when we read them. The book of Judges ends with Israel in total religious, social and moral chaos. They show us exactly what happens when people push God aside and try to rule their own lives.

64 – BROTHER AGAINST BROTHER
Read verse 10 again
"Give them what they deserve!" (v 10) They were furious at what happened, but totally failed to recognise their own sin and rejection against God. Can you understand why God didn't give them immediate success in punishing their "evil" neighbours? It's all very well weeping before the Lord as thousands of their men are mown down, but what about weeping for their own sin?

119

65 – LEAVE ME ALONE

The Israelites were losing in battle but they still trusted God to give them victory and turned to Him for help.

Read Hebrews 10 v 19–25

▶ *What can Christians hold on to in the dark times?*

▶ *What gives us the confidence and ability to approach God? (v19)*

▶ *Why can we hold on to this hope? (v23)*

▶ *What should it lead to? (v24)*

▶ *What else should we do, to help us keep going? (v25)*

66 – EDGE OF EXTINCTION

So what was the situation for God's people by the end of Judges? Well, God's people were living in God's place, Canaan. But as for living under His rule, forget it. So, God's promises to Abraham were not fulfilled in Judges. God's plan to bring His people together in His place to live perfectly under His rule isn't completed at this point. So what are the lessons for us from Judges then?

Firstly, about God. The only hero of the book. Amazingly, He carries on looking after His people. Think of the ways He does that — in judgment, rescue, discipline, control, even leaving them to their own devices.

▶ *What has Judges taught you about what God is like?*

Secondly, the judges themselves. God

raised them up and equipped them with His Spirit to bring victory for His people. Which lasted for a while. Compare God's ultimate, eternal rescue through Jesus.

Lastly, God's people. They're called to obey and trust Him. Jesus Christ's rescue broke the power of sin, that vicious circle. So ask Him to help you get rid of sin and live for Him alone.

▶ *Will you do what you think is right, or what God says?*

Judges is a downward spiral, but we've had hints of a king to come. God's purpose and plans continued — He *would* send a king to rescue His people and bring them back to Himself.

PSALMS

67 – PRAISE AND PANIC

Read verses 4–10 again

David remembered great things God had done for the Israelites — rescuing them from Egypt (v6), leading them through the desert (v7) to Canaan (v10). And Sinai (v8) — the time God drew close to His people and gave them the 10 Commandments.

▶ *What stands out about God in these verses?*

Now read verse 18 and then Ephesians 4 v 7–16

▶ *Who has given what to who? (v7–8)*

▶ *Why is Christian teaching so important? (v11–13)*

- ▶ *What's the ultimate goal? (v13)*
- ▶ *What do we need to watch out for? (v14)*
- ▶ *How can we avoid such dangers? (v15)*
- ▶ *How does the church ("the body of Christ") grow? (v16)*

68 – PRAY WHEN YOU'RE SINKING
**Read verse 9 again
and then John 2 v 12–22**

- ▶ *What caused Jesus to react the way He did? (v14, v16)*
- ▶ *Does Jesus' passionate anger surprise you? Why / why not?*
- ▶ *What did the disciples recall from Psalm 69? (v17)*
- ▶ *What did the Jews want? (v18)*
- ▶ *What was Jesus' surprising answer, and the Jews' response? (v19–20)*
- ▶ *John gives us an editorial note to help us. What is it? (v21–22)*

Even more than David, Jesus was mocked for defending God and His house, the temple. And He went through much worse persecution on the way to dying on the cross for us.

69 – QUICK! HELP!
Read Psalm 40 v 11–17

- ▶ *Why did David need God's help? (v12)*
- ▶ *What does David want? (v14–15)*
- ▶ *What else? (v16)*

Verses 16–17 show us David's different moods — his praise to God, his reliance on God, his cry for help. Spend time with God now, thanking Him for specific things; committing yourself to serving Him; asking Him to help you with anything that's weighing on your mind.

70 – SENIOR MOMENT
Write your own version of Psalm 71, with a verse/paragraph for each of these things:

1. Ask God to keep you safe and bring you through tough times.
2. Remember what God has done for you in the past.
3. Spill out the worries you have on your mind.
4. Detail how you'll tell people about the Lord.
5. Praise God.

71 – DOUBLE VISION
Read Isaiah 11 v 1–9

- ▶ *How is the coming King (Jesus) described here?*
  v2:
  v3–4:
  v5:
- ▶ *And what will life be like when He rules eternally? (v6–9)*

Yep, you guessed it — time for more prayer and praise and thanks.

121

ACTS

72 – TO BE CONTINUED...

The devil was defeated at the cross but he is not yet destroyed. We don't need to be scared but we do need to be on our guard against his attacks.

Check out these Bible bits to get the big picture:
Acts 2 v 34–36,
Revelation 12 v 10–12,
1 Peter 5 v 8–9,
Ephesians 6 v 10–20,
Romans 16 v 20,
Revelation 20 v 10.

73 – PLAN A

Does your Bible have footnotes telling you where every Old Testament quote comes from? If not, get hold of a Bible that does and skim through a gospel or two to see how often we see Jesus fulfilling God's pre-ordained plan of salvation. Take a look at **Isaiah 53** and **Psalm 22 v 1–18** while you're at it.

In Jerusalem, Peter repeatedly told his listeners: "You killed Jesus, God raised Him and we're witnesses." Now Paul says about Jesus' hearers: "They killed Jesus, God raised Him and there are witnesses." See? Jesus' death and resurrection are always the key bits to talk about. Don't get deflected and distracted. Many conversations about Christian stuff seem difficult or impossible or random. Bring it back to Jesus!

74 – A PROMISE AND A CHOICE

Imagine someone asked you: *"Why is the resurrection so important?"* What would you say?

Read 1 Corinthians 15 and jot down a list of reasons why the resurrection is so crucial to the Christian faith.

75 – SHARE AND BEWARE

Does it discourage you when you face opposition for being a Christian? It's hardly surprising and it's not exactly fun! Get your head around these passages and pray that you would build your foundations on them:
Matthew 16 v 24–26,
Mark 3 v 20–21,
Mark 10 v 29–30,
Romans 8 v 17,
Philippians 1 v 29,
1 Peter 2 v 21.

76 – GOSPEL UNITED

▶ *Why do you think the good news about Jesus has such a dramatic effect?*

Look at v1–2 again,
then read 1 Corinthians 1 v 18–30
and 2 Corinthians 2 v 14–16.
▶ *How does that help you to understand it?*

77 – HEARD IT ALL BEFORE

Some things are non-negotiable when telling others about Jesus — God as Creator and King, our sin and rebellion, Jesus' rescue through His death and resurrection and of course His return as Judge.

But you might start in very different places with different people. How might you begin a conversation with a friend who:

a) doesn't believe in God.
b) believes there are many gods and different paths to heaven.
c) says you can't be sure about anything spiritual.
d) thinks being good will get them into heaven.

78 – RETURN JOURNEY

You've just witnessed *Paul's first missionary journey*. Check your Bible to see if there's a map which shows the route. If so, from Acts, check what happened in each place and see how much ground Paul and Barnabas covered.

79 – THE GREAT DEBATE

Read verse 1 again

Antioch was in Galatia. Paul wrote a great letter to these Christians in Galatia, touching on the same topic.

Read Galatians 3 v 1–9

ⓘ *What was Paul shocked about? (v2–3)*
ⓘ *What's the answer to v5?*
ⓘ *What has always been the right*

response to God? (v6–7)
ⓘ *What was God's plan all along? (v8–9)*

The law says: "You must do this" (as every human religion does). But the gospel says: "Jesus has done it all". What rules have people told you to follow in order to be a "real" or "serious" Christian?

ⓘ *What's likely to cause you to take your eyes off the gospel?*
ⓘ *What would make Paul call you a "foolish" Christian?*

80 – THE GREAT DEBATE PART II

You might have no trouble avoiding eating blood or strangled animals (unless you had black pudding or blood sausage for breakfast — eeek!) but how are you doing on keeping free from idols (possessions, appearance, money, popularity etc) and staying sexually pure? Ask for God's help where you find these things difficult.

81 – BARNA' SPLIT

Mark might have left the work early but he went on to write the Gospel of Mark, which has been a huge blessing to Christians through the ages. Silas and Paul made a great team too — check out not only the rest of Acts but also 2 Corinthians 1 v 19, 1 Thessalonians 1 v 1, 2 Thessalonians 1 v 1 and 1 Peter 5 v 12.

Thank God that He uses us despite our weakness. Indeed His strength is made perfect in our weakness!

ZEPHANIAH
God's day

82 – DAYS OF WARNING

The prophet's job was to call God's people back to His covenant — His promise to give them a great life when they obey His laws. God's promise to destroy isn't unreasonable; it's entirely in line with that covenant and with His character.

▶ If God didn't punish wrong, what would that tell us about Him?
▶ Why were His people to be punished more severely?
▶ What's the warning here for us?

83 – DAY OF TERROR

Read verses 8–9 again

The punishment on those wearing foreign clothes isn't race hatred. Foreign clothes = those who had chosen to follow the ways of other nations and to worship their gods.

Those who avoid stepping on the threshold (entrance) (v 9) is literally: those who skip or leap over the threshold. In 1 Samuel 5 v 5 we learn that Philistine priests avoided stepping on the threshold of the temple. Now Israel's priests do the same. Like their politicians, they follow the ways of idol worshippers.

84 – DOOM'S DAY

The idea of a "remnant" appears again and again in the Old Testament.

Read Jeremiah 23 v 3–4,
Micah 2 v 12–13,
and Micah 5 v 7–9

God's judgment against the sin of His people would be so devastating that only a few survivors, a remnant, would remain.

▶ How does this fact reveal both God's love and His anger?
▶ What makes it exciting that God does keep a remnant?

86 – DAY OF HOPE

Read 2 Peter 3 v 8–13

▶ Why does God delay His judgment day? (v8–9)
▶ What will that day be like? (v10)
▶ How should we get ready? (v11–12)

When the world ends, Christians are going to get a new home, the *"home of righteousness"*. It will be an awesome place with no selfishness, depression or death. A place where we'll be overcome with how great and loving God is. A place to get excited about.

PSALMS

87 – SENSE OF PERSPECTIVE

Read verse 6 and then
Proverbs 1 v 8–9, 3 v 3 and 3 v 21–22

▶ What should we replace pride with?
▶ What are you overly proud about?
▶ How can you be more humble?

Read Psalm 73 v 18–20

The psalm writer sees that God is in control of all that's happening around him. He is aware of the wicked and holds their future in His hands. No one can stand against God. Look at verse 20 — when God destroys His enemies, they'll vanish like the shadowy characters of a dream.

88 – TEMPLE OF GLOOM

The story of Jerusalem's destruction by the Babylonians is told in 2 Kings 23–25.

Read 2 Kings 23 v 36 – 24 v 4

Babylon was the new superpower at the time, replacing Assyria.

▶ *But who was it that sent forces to destroy Judah? (v2–3)*

▶ *What does this tell us about God's role in history?*

Read 2 Kings 24 v 10–20

This was the beginning of the end for Judah and Jerusalem. Only farm workers were left (v14). Anyone who might organise trouble was taken away.

▶ *What was the reason for all this? (v20)*

Read 2 Kings chapter 25

Jerusalem and its leaders were killed, the city was trashed and the temple (the sign of God's presence with His people) was burned to the ground. Anyone who joined the revolution was beheaded. Everyone else was taken away to captivity in Babylon.

At the end, we're told that Judah's last king, Jehoiachin, was freed from prison in Babylon after 37 years. So what? Well, God had promised not to wipe out the line of King David. The story of God and His people, despite this shattering judgment, would go on. And it would be truly resurrected in Jesus.

90 – THE FEAR

Use Psalms 73–76 to write your own song/poem/prayer to the Lord.

- Rewrite Psalm 73 v 23–26 in your own words.
- Use Psalm 74 v 12–17 to celebrate God's greatness.
- And Psalm 75 to pray for justice.
- Then Psalm 76 to praise God for His power and recognise His terrifying but fair judgment.
- Finish off with bits of Psalm 67, to praise God positively.

engage wants to hear from YOU!

▶ Share experiences of God at work in your life
▶ Any questions you have about the Bible or the Christian life?
▶ How can we make *engage* better?

Email us — **martin@thegoodbook.co.uk**

(Unlike in previous issues, this email address actually works!)

Or use the space below to write us a quick note. You can post it to:

engage 37 Elm Road, New Malden, Surrey, KT3 3HB, UK

In the next engage

Isaiah City of dreams
2 Thessalonians Ready, steady, grow
1 Samuel Kingdom come
Acts Visions, prisons and riots
Plus: How to share your faith
Isn't the Bible out of date?
Real life stories
What is the gospel?

Order engage now!

Make sure you order the next issue of **engage**. Or even better, grab a one-year subscription to make sure **engage** lands in your hands as soon as it's out.

Call us to order in the UK on 0345 225 0880
International: +44 (0) 20 8942 0880

or visit your friendly neighbourhood website:
UK: www.thegoodbook.co.uk
N America: www.thegoodbook.com
Australia: www.thegoodbook.com.au
New Zealand: www.thegoodbook.co.nz

Growing with God

Faithful, contemporary Bible reading resources for every age and stage.

NEW!

Beginning with God
For pre-schoolers

Table Talk & XTB
Table Talk for 4-11s and their parents, *XTB* for 7-11s

Discover
For 11-13s

Engage
For 14-18s

Explore
For adults

All Good Book Company Bible reading resources...

- have a strong focus on practical application
- encourage people to read the Bible for themselves
- explain Bible passages in context
- cover Bible books in the Old and New Testament

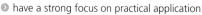

UK: www.thegoodbook.co.uk
N America: www.thegoodbook.com
Australia: www.thegoodbook.com.au
New Zealand: www.thegoodbook.co.nz

the**good**book
COMPANY